Nightingale

Animal
Series editor: Jonathan Burt

Already published

Albatross Graham Barwell · *Ant* Charlotte Sleigh · *Ape* John Sorenson · *Badger* Daniel Heath Justice
Bat Tessa Laird · *Bear* Robert E. Bieder · *Beaver* Rachel Poliquin · *Bedbug* Klaus Reinhardt
Bee Claire Preston · *Beetle* Adam Dodd · *Bison* Desmond Morris · *Camel* Robert Irwin
Cat Katharine M. Rogers · *Chicken* Annie Potts · *Cockroach* Marion Copeland · *Cow* Hannah Velten
Crab Cynthia Chris · *Crocodile* Dan Wylie · *Crow* Boria Sax · *Deer* John Fletcher · *Dog* Susan McHugh
Dolphin Alan Rauch · *Donkey* Jill Bough · *Duck* Victoria de Rijke · *Eagle* Janine Rogers · *Eel* Richard
Schweid · *Elephant* Dan Wylie · *Falcon* Helen Macdonald · *Flamingo* Caitlin R. Kight · *Fly* Steven
Connor · *Fox* Martin Wallen · *Frog* Charlotte Sleigh · *Giraffe* Edgar Williams · *Goat* Joy Hinson
Goldfish Anna Marie Roos · *Gorilla* Ted Gott and Kathryn Weir · *Guinea Pig* Dorothy Yamamoto
Hare Simon Carnell · *Hedgehog* Hugh Warwick · *Hippopotamus* Edgar Williams · *Horse* Elaine Walker
Human Amanda Rees and Charlotte Sleigh · *Hyena* Mikita Brottman · *Jellyfish* Peter Williams
Kangaroo John Simons · *Kingfisher* Ildiko Szabo · *Leech* Robert G. W. Kirk and Neil Pemberton
Leopard Desmond Morris · *Lion* Deirdre Jackson · *Lizard* Boria Sax · *Llama* Helen Cowie
Lobster Richard J. Kin · *Mole* Steve Gronert Ellerhoff · *Monkey* Desmond Morris · *Moose* Kevin Jackson
Mosquito Richard Jones · *Moth* Matthew Gandy · *Mouse* Georgie Carroll · *Nightingale* Bethan Roberts
Octopus Richard Schweid · *Ostrich* Edgar Williams · *Otter* Daniel Allen · *Owl* Desmond Morris
Oyster Rebecca Stott · *Parrot* Paul Carter · *Peacock* Christine E. Jackson · *Pelican* Barbara Allen
Penguin Stephen Martin · *Pig* Brett Mizelle · *Pigeon* Barbara Allen · *Polar Bear* Margery Fee
Rabbit Victoria Dickinson · *Raccoon* Daniel Heath Justice · *Rat* Jonathan Burt · *Rhinoceros* Kelly Enright
Salmon Peter Coates · *Sardine* Trevor Day · *Scorpion* Louise M. Pryke · *Seal* Victoria Dickenson
Shark Dean Crawford · *Sheep* Philip Armstrong · *Skunk* Alyce Miller · *Snail* Peter Williams
Snake Drake Stutesman · *Sparrow* Kim Todd · *Spider* Katarzyna and Sergiusz Michalski · *Squid* Martin
Wallen · *Swallow* Angela Turner · *Swan* Peter Young · *Tiger* Susie Green · *Tortoise* Peter Young
Trout James Owen · *Turtle* Louise M. Pryke · *Vulture* Thom van Dooren · *Walrus* John Miller
and Louise Miller · *Wasp* Richard Jones · *Whale* Joe Roman · *Wild Boar* Dorothy Yamamoto
Wolf Garry Marvin · *Woodpecker* Gerard Gorman · *Zebra* Christopher Plumb and Samuel Shaw

Nightingale

Bethan Roberts

REAKTION BOOKS

For my Mum and Dad

Published by
REAKTION BOOKS LTD
Unit 32, Waterside
44–48 Wharf Road
London N1 7UX, UK
www.reaktionbooks.co.uk

First published 2021
Copyright © Bethan Roberts 2021

Printed and bound in India by Replika Press Pvt. Ltd

A catalogue record for this book is available from the British Library

ISBN 978 1 78914 474 1

Contents

Introduction: 'No Better Dress than Russet Brown'

Nature's jazzman, forest muse, scrub skulker, little brown job: the nightingale is a contradictory bird. Notoriously reclusive, and known for singing under the cover of darkness, it has inspired more poems and paeans than any other wild creature on earth. A small, relatively plain bird, its appearance and near invisibility are at odds with the vividness of the cultural life that has been spun from its celebrated song. As John Clare writes in his 1832 poem 'The Nightingales [*sic*] Nest',

> . . . Ive nestled down
> And watched her while she sung – and her renown
> Hath made me marvel that so famed a bird
> Should have no better dress than russet brown.[1]

Or, as the naturalist James Bolton has it in his 1794 *Essay on British Song Birds*, 'Not only in the time of Pliny, but long before him, and since, down to this day, this poor bird has been the butt of whining lovers, theatrical writers, romancers, novelists, poets, poetasters, and liars of many other denominations.'[2]

For, as well as the most versified bird, the nightingale is also the most mythologized: what we might think of as the 'real' bird has been obscured and superseded by myriad associations, symbols, metaphors and myths. Our propensity towards attaching

Nightingale singing in Pulborough Brooks, Sussex.

7

human emotions and stories to aspects of the natural world reaches new heights in the nightingale. The bird, as we have made it, has taken on an almost-mythological status, such that we might question where the 'real' nightingale can be found, if at all: in its natural habitat or in the pages of literary history. This book roves across more than 2,000 years of nature and culture with this question in mind. It considers how this bird, more than any other, muddies the distinction between the two realms, calls into question the category of the 'real' and tests the very limits of human comprehension and expression.

There are two species of nightingale: an Old World passerine bird, the common nightingale (*Luscinia megarhynchos*), which breeds in Western and Central Europe and northern Africa; and the lesser-known thrush nightingale (*Luscinia luscinia*), also known as the sprosser, of Northern and Eastern Europe. The species are very similar in appearance and behaviour; it is difficult to distinguish between the two. This book is concerned mainly with the common nightingale, for that is the species famed throughout cultural history, yet its northeasterly relative is still simply 'the nightingale' – and similarly loaded with meaning – to those who know it. Vladimir Nabokov recalled hearing the bird in the bathroom of the family country house, and dedicated his youthful verse to it; it is also heard with suggestive resonance in Soviet filmmaker Andrei Tarkovsky's historical masterpiece *Andrei Rublev* (1966).

While it has attracted many accolades as a musician, the nightingale has more often been celebrated in poetry, and as a poet. In his *Natural History* (AD 77–9), Pliny the Elder notes that at the birth of the first lyric poet Stesichorus (*c.* 630–555 BC), a nightingale flew to his lips and sang there. In ancient Greek, the word *aedon* means both nightingale and poet, and at the height of Romanticism, the literary movement which prized the nightingale more

than any other, P. B. Shelley declared that 'A poet is a nightingale who sits in darkness, and sings to cheer its own solitude with sweet sounds.'[3] The focus on the nightingale as expressive in its song has prompted countless explorations of poetic voice that build to the crescendo of John Keats's 'Ode to a Nightingale' (1819), which is perhaps the best-known poem written in the English language. As such, the nightingale's place in literature has become an integral part of what this bird *is*, far beyond the important associations of, say, the cuckoo, robin or skylark. Nightingale verse is a fascinating record of the changing relationship between poetry and the natural world over the centuries, yet it is, at the same time and in many ways, unrepresentative of it, inscribing as it does the unique hold this bird has had over the poetic imagination. For poets, to write about the nightingale is often a test of poetic skill and vocation, to inherit and find a way into the most loaded of literary conversations. Nightingale poems are often about these things – about poetry itself.

There is a surprising lack of folk- and oral lore – which is vast on other celebrated species – about the nightingale, the fame of which is owed almost wholly to poets.[4] Where the nightingale does appear in country traditions, it is usually in relation to its arrival with the spring (the bird overwinters in Africa and arrives in its breeding territories in April–May). An old saying is that 'On the third of April the cuckoo and the nightingale arrive,' and because of the coincidence of their arrival, the nightingale is often associated with the cuckoo. In Ukraine, to hear the nightingale before the cuckoo foretells a good summer, but if the nightingale comes after the cuckoo, times will be hard. According to another superstition, to hear the nightingale before the cuckoo signals luck in love. The nightingale is known as the 'barley bird' in East Anglia in England, because its song is first heard when barley is being sown (although the name has been given elsewhere to several other birds). In Kent, England, there is a saying that when the nightingales arrive early and sing well, fruit crops will be good. In Sussex, it is said that the bluebells wait for the singing of the

Ryūryūkyo Shinsai, *New Moon; Nightingale on a Plum Branch*, Japan, 19th century.

Nightingale in a garden from a fresco in Pompeii, 1st century AD.

nightingales before flowering. The bird is also variously associated with the violet, cowslip and daffodil. In Japan, the nightingale, *uguisu*, sings sweet songs of spring joy among the bamboo and plum trees, and there is a Korean court dance, dating back to the 1400s, called *Ch'unaengjŏn*, which literally means 'Spring Nightingale Dance'. The nightingale as a bird of spring underpins much poetry, too. 'The messenger of spring, the sweet voiced nightingale', Sappho, poet of ancient Greece, writes, while in the *Parliament of*

Fowls, Geoffrey Chaucer's nightingale 'clepeth forth the grene leves newe'.[5] In Persian poetry, the nightingale sings during *mawsem-e gol*, season of roses, and Keats's poem is infused with the scent of 'mid-May's eldest child, The / coming musk-rose'.[6]

The nightingale as bird of the spring is one of its few accurate poetic associations, for it is in its poetic life that this bird has been mythologized through and through. Most often, the singing nightingale has been depicted as female, as melancholic and as singing only at night. In the natural world it is the male bird that sings to attract a mate and to defend territory, and it sings by both day and night. The source of much nightingale misapprehension is the Philomela myth – originally a Greek myth but formalized in literary history by the Roman poet Ovid in his *Metamorphoses* (AD 8). This hugely popular and influential work has seen the nightingale endlessly reworked and recycled as Philomela, the raped young woman who was transformed by the gods into a nightingale.

In his 1798 poem 'The Nightingale', Samuel Taylor Coleridge pinpoints the source of the association between the nightingale and melancholy to one 'night-wandering man' (they have a lot to answer for),

> whose heart was pierc'd
> With the remembrance of a grievous wrong,
> Or slow distemper, or neglected love,
> (And so, poor Wretch! fill'd all things with himself
> And made all gentle sounds tell back the tale
> Of his own sorrows) he and such as he
> First nam'd these notes a melancholy strain;
> And many a poet echoes the conceit.[7]

As Coleridge points out, the resonances of birdsong are necessarily and intensely subjective, all too often steeped in the

remembrances and temper of the listener. In 1885 the Reverend C. A. Johns noted that 'It's a disputed point whether the nightingale's song can be considered joyous or melancholy. This must always remain a question of taste.'[8] His own opinion was that 'the piteous wailing note which is its characteristic nature casts a shade of sadness over the whole song, even those portions which gush with the most exuberant gladness.'[9] Yet, to D. H. Lawrence,

The nightingale . . . is the most unsad thing in the world; even more unsad than the peacock full of gleam. He has nothing to be sad about. He feels perfect with life. It isn't conceit. He just feels life-perfect, and he trills it out – shouts, jugs, gurgles, trills, gives long, mock-plaintiff calls, makes declarations, assertions, triumphs; but he never reflects. It is pure music, in so far as you could never put words to it.[10]

The nightingale might not reflect, but countless poets, nature writers and musicologists have reflected on it and found plenty to be sad about, musing on that 'pure music' and endeavouring to put words to it and make words work for it.

As Coleridge's poem also divines, the nightingale's song has certainly given rise to many of the bird's cultural associations: night is the time both of loving and of illicit meetings, of melancholy and sleep-deprived wanderings (one may lead to the other, Coleridge's poem suggests). Etymologically, 'nightingale' means 'night singer' (Old English *galan* is 'to sing'). The Latin *lusciniola* is from *luscinia*, 'singing in the twilight'.[11] The key to what is thought to be the earliest nightingale poem in our language, an Old English riddle, lies in the description of the bird as an 'evening songster'.[12] Showing the power of a name, and how we can run away with our own labelling of the natural world, the belief that the nightingale sings only at night has been widespread. It is much found in works by William Shakespeare. In *Romeo and Juliet* (1597), the eponymous lovers use the bird as a clock to judge when their night-time meeting must end. As Juliet complains,

Wilt thou be gone? It is not yet near day.
It was the nightingale, and not the lark,
That pierced the fear-full hollow of thine ear.

Nightly she sings on yon pom'granate tree.
Believe me, love, it was the nightingale.[13]

The bird has soundtracked many a lover's tryst, with the lark the nightingale's inverse: herald of morning and curtailer of the night's various pleasures and torments.

In *The Merchant of Venice*, Portia puts the popularity of the bird's song down entirely to its night-time performance:

. . . I think,
The nightingale, if she should sing by day,
When every goose is cackling, would be thought
No better a musician than the wren.[14]

While the nightingale may sing both day and night, its song at night-time, when very few birds do sing, is certainly key to its

Nightingale sitting on a branch in a forest. Coloured wood engraving by Josiah Wood Whymper (1813–1903).

A nightingale sings by moonlight.

magic. Spooling up out of the darkness, when all else is hushed by the night, the song is incredibly loud, enhanced by muted sight and carrying further on the cooler air (it can carry up to a mile, or 2 km). Isaak Walton said that they who hear the nightingale at midnight 'might well be lifted above earth, and say, Lord, what music hast thou provided for the Saints in Heaven, when thou affordest bad men such music on earth!'[15]

The bird has often been heard as a foretaste of heaven, as singing in harmony with its sounds, and, indeed, one way in which I have interpreted the song – and the power it wields – is as an aural equivalent of a 'thin place' (usually sacred sites, such as places of worship and ritual), where the veil between this world and another is at its thinnest.[16]

The nightingale is not quite universally loved, however, especially by those trying to get a good night's sleep: 'Leaf-loving nightingales, loquacious sex, / Sleep quietly, I beg, and cease your din,' a poet in the *Greek Anthology*, a collection of poems dating from the seventh century BC to AD 1000, implores.[17] More vehement is the 'The Anti-nightingale Song' in the eleventh-century collection of poems *Cambridge Songs*, in which the nightingale is

Royal Mail
nightingale stamp
from *Songbirds*
series (2017).

a blaring 'woodland prostitute'.[18] 'Will you never stop that racket, / overrated little bird?' the speaker wonders.[19] Others have hurled a shoe at the incessant bird, while, to Sir Edward Grey, writing in *The Charm of Birds* (1927), the nightingale's song is one 'to listen to, but not to live with'.[20]

I am often asked about my own experience of hearing the nightingale. Like others, I don't have the words to describe the sound, but I know how it feels. I first heard one as an adult and, with a head full of Romantic poetry, I expected to wonder at the bird through Keats and others. Yet, there in the green and dark, all else falls away: that moment, the song and sound, and nothing else. The shock of the volume and variety, everything is more sudden by the moment that the nightingale's song seems to have the power to pull into being. I have never felt such an intense presence than when hearing this bird, and there's a purity of experience that comes with that. All birdsong sounds wholly pure, yet the deep presence-pull of the nightingale's song is nature's purity in an enriched and rarefied form. The astonishment of hearing the nightingale feels close to overwhelming yet it never tips over the edge, and perhaps the song's dance upon that edge is part of the giddy joy. Most of all, the experience is steeped in a sense of not quite being able to grasp what is being heard, of something beyond: the other side of the thin place. Ears and comprehension work differently (and this is enhanced by darkness) – reaching and striving yet all too often spinning and reeling, losing a hold on that protean sound by each moment's rush. This sensation is something that I will return to, for it is one thing of which the research of this book has helped me make sense. However, this book isn't about what I think or feel; I'd like for it to be a guidebook of sorts, which might help readers work out their own sense of this bird.

The – with apologies – Englishness of much of this book reflects the peculiar obsession the nation has with a bird that visits the country for only a few months of the year, and sings for not much more than six weeks. This, together with the nightingale's secretiveness and night-time song, has no doubt fuelled the madness. As Richard Mabey writes in his splendid *Book of Nightingales* (1997) – an odyssey to locate the bird through poetry, ornithology and his own brand of personal romanticism: 'This virtual disembodiment has helped to make their song the equivalent of a psychologist's ink-blot test, capable of carrying all kinds of meaning, and has heightened its ambivalence.'[21]

Nightingale singing in Volkspark Hasenheide, Berlin.

To Mark Cocker, the invisible nightingale's song of darkness is comparable with the daylight melody of the lark (the second-most-versified bird in history), similarly difficult to see singing high over open territories: 'A birdsong without an apparent author has lent itself to the human imagination as the most plastic of symbols.'[22] It is not entirely clear why the nightingale sings at night, but it is thought to be due to decreased competition and the fact that the female birds migrate at this time. Wladyslaw Starewicz's pioneering stop-motion film *La voix du rossignol* (Voice of the Nightingale, 1923) offers a different explanation. The film tells the story of a little girl who catches a nightingale in a trap and keeps it as her plaything. Through its song, she comes to realize that the bird has a life of its own and releases it. The nightingale is reunited with its mate, and in gratitude loans the little girl its voice as a reward for her kindness, remaining silent during the day and only at night, 'when little children are asleep does he regain his beautiful voice'.

Also arising out of its nightly activity, wakefulness is often perceived as a distinctive quality of the nightingale. 'To rest as much as the nightingale' was once a proverbial expression denoting a very bad sleeper, and in classical times, the flesh of the nightingale was eaten to aid wakefulness. An old European folk-tale told of the nightingale and the blindworm. Each has only one eye, and one day the nightingale steals the eye of the blindworm before heading off to a wedding. The blindworm vows to catch the nightingale asleep and recover its eye, and ever since the nightingale has sung by night in order to stay awake. Ambrose of Milan (d. 397) attributes the nightingale's wakefulness to more maternal activity. In his *Hexaemeron*, Ambrose describes the bird as an ever-watchful guardian, consoling herself through the long sleepless night with her sweet song and encouraging her eggs to hatch by it.

La voix du rossignol (The Voice of the Nightingale, 1923), dir. Wladyslaw Starewicz.

20

As John Clare points out, the appearance of the nightingale – an 'LBJ' (little brown job) in birding terms – contrasts with the colourful weave of culture to which its song has given rise. The bird's plainness is noted in the earliest nightingale poems. In a riddle-like poem by Bishop Aldhelm (d. 709/10) the nightingale proclaims, 'For all that I am dusky in colour, yet I am not to be scorned for my singing.'[23] A century or so later, one of the insults levelled at the nightingale by the owl in the Middle English debate poem *The Owl and the Nightingale* is, 'You're a dim and dirty colour; and you look just like a little, sooty ball.'[24] Some fabulists have sought to account for the bird's plainness. In one folk-tale, God, deeming the birds he had created too plain, decides to paint

Nightingales in Suffolk wearing rings that can be tracked.

them. The ever-retiring nightingale comes last, when the paint has all but run out. God instructs the nightingale to open its mouth and places a drop of gold paint on its tongue, blessing it – while its dress might remain dull – with a beautiful song.

Unsurprisingly, due to its plain appearance, the nightingale has not attracted much attention in visual art: praise and mimicry of its song is better suited to poetry and music. Where the bird does appear, other aspects and meanings often compensate for its plainness: the moon, or the rich symbolism of nightingale and rose, *gol-o-bolbol*, a mainstay of decorative Persian art. The best-known nightingale artwork is Max Ernst's collage *Two Children Are Threatened by a Nightingale* (1924), one of the founding works

Binding of a divan of Hafiz, 1842, Iran, showing a nightingale and rose.

of Surrealism, the tenets of which – mystery, irrationality – colour the piece. In the work, the nightingale is seen flying against the sky over two figures: a girl wielding a long knife and a supine figure. Another figure, holding a child atop a miniature house, reaches out to the frame of the collage to press a button, as if to escape from its nightmarish world. (Ernst suggested the piece was inspired by the death of his sister.) The wooden gate also mounted onto the frame dramatizes the portal-like effect of the work: it appears to offer us access to an interior world, from which its inhabitants seek to escape. Indeed, the piece presents a psychological scene, rather than a real landscape, and there is little of the nightingale to be seen or felt within it. This is a bird of the mind – but then perhaps all nightingales are.

The quality that has been most celebrated in the nightingale's song is its variety. This was noted in a well-known passage by Pliny in his *Natural History* (with more recent musical terms creeping into the translation):

> The sound is given out with modulations . . . now varied by managing the breath, now made staccato by checking it, or linked together by prolonging it, or carried on by holding it back; or it is suddenly lowered, and at times sinks into a mere murmur, loud, low, a bass, treble, with trills, with long notes, modulated when this seems good – soprano, mezzo, baritone.[25]

The bird's variety holds another clue to the identity of the speaker in the Old English nightingale riddle: 'I've one mouth but many voices; / I dissemble and often change my tune.'[26] One of the Arabic names for the nightingale is *hazār-dāstān* – teller of a thousand tales – in reference to the bird's virtuosity. Studies have shown that one male nightingale has a repertoire of around

Max Ernst,
*Two Children
Are Threatened
by a Nightingale*,
1924, oil with
painted wood.

24

250 phrases, and a single singer may deliver up to four hundred phrases per hour, with each series of phrases differing either in its introduction or the sequence in which it is followed. Until recently, studies put the total number of nightingale phrases to around six hundred, yet an ongoing citizen science project in Berlin is exploding this figure. Berliners are asked to record nightingales via an app, Naturblick, and the research group has identified 2,300 different phrases – a figure which is anticipated to rise.

The nightingale's virtuosity has provided a challenge to musicians and composers who have sought to recreate it, while those who have described the nightingale's song in words have frequently turned to the language of music, a man-made art, as recourse. This can be seen in Pliny's description, which concludes that the bird has 'consummate knowledge of music', and makes use of 'all the devices in that tiny throat which human science has devised with all the elaborate mechanism of the flute'.[27] More recently, Richard Mabey describes a nightingale's 'performance':

> He is louder and more extravagant now, and seems to be rehearsing the whole nightingale repertoire. He sings a stylish four-note phrase, then repeats it in a minor key. He slides into a bubbling tremolo on a single note and holds it for more than ten seconds. How does he breathe? I cannot believe he is not consciously improvising.[28]

Recalling Pliny, the description is live and alive, on location (there by the stream at the edge of a fen wood), a present-tense evocation of the experience of hearing. Yet, at the same time, the description is distanced from nightingale nature through the cultural filters of both language and music. In an article in *The Guardian*, Mabey reflected on the description:

In retrospect I didn't get it quite right. I'm not sure I should have tried to describe the song in the language of human music . . . In short, I think I was too self-conscious. Yet trying not to be would have written me – a self-aware human – out of the relationship. Squaring that circle is the heart of the problem, in fact the heart of all our ecological problems.[29]

Writing about the nightingale seems to bring into focus the complexities of writing nature, not least because the nightingale has persistently been considered as a creature that touches the realm of musical expression and conscious creation in its song. As Mabey finds, there do not seem to be the words to reach it outside of the human terms of artistry and performance. Often there do not seem to be the words at all. This is partly why the nightingale has inspired such a wealth of material, perhaps: the bird presents nature's supreme challenge to writers. The nightingale is poised between source of inspiration as the creature that is most like us in its perceived ability to create, to express joy and sorrow, and as nature's triumph over us, driving artists like a madness in their pursuit to match or capture it, sometimes to master and beat it.

As Mabey writes, there is no 'squaring that circle', and human culture and experience inevitably mediate between us and the birds with whom we share this planet. This mediation begins at the level of language, and it blooms in myriad forms across science, poetry, music and lore. It is a fact of humanness, as we make sense of – some would say make – our world, but what does it do to our relationship with said world? Does it take us closer to, or push us apart from other species? At the most basic level, we need to be able to put language to a bird, to name it, in order to know and then to love it, yet how far should we take our words?

Some see the investment of birds with symbolic meaning as 'exploitative', taking us far from a bird's truth, while others see this 'nature capture [as] a species of love'.[30] Again, these are particularly vexed questions to ask of a nightingale, especially when much of what has been written about the bird is factually incorrect. Does ornithological inaccuracy and the huge weight of symbolism lose the nightingale to us? Or does this tendency to

Nightingale engraving by Oscar Dressler, in Eugenio Bettoni's *Storia naturale degli uccelli che nidificano in Lombardia* (Natural History of Birds that Nest in Lombardy, 1865).

mythologize foster love and kinship? This book seeks to capture the swell of closeness and distance, love and loss, that has been rendered ever differently throughout cultural history. One thing is certain: through its unique place in poetic history, the nightingale – perhaps more than any other creature – shows how closely, how inseparably, nature and culture are intertwined.

Despite all our poems about and our cherishing of the nightingale, it is disappearing from its British breeding territories: the bird has declined more than 90 per cent in these areas over the last fifty years, and its range has contracted by 43 per cent. The contradictory presence–absence of the nightingale, with which this introduction opened, is being realized differently for the current age. While it may be vanishing from our wood and scrublands, the reclusive nightingale has, in a sense, never been more visible: the threat to the bird has provoked a cultural call to arms in a new

Nightingale from Francis Orpen Morris, *A History of British Birds* (1851–7). Woodcut by Benjamin Fawcett.

reworking of nature–culture interrelations. The nightingale reveals not only the extent to which our views of birds have been shaped by poetry, but the implications this can have for their conservation.

The foci and organization of this book have been led by the material, and it is for this reason that there are two chapters on literary history (a book on the literary life of the nightingale could fill ten volumes), and none on visual art. It is hoped that readers will find their own way through a history of nightingale art in the illustrations. As noted, it is one that is often bound up with the bird's literary history, yet moments in the history of bird engraving do capture the richness and beauty of the brown-cream, russet-tinged hues of the bird, such as the hand-coloured wood-engravings and lithographs of Benjamin Fawcett and Elizabeth Gould. Chapter One outlines the bird's natural history – by which all must be measured – and how that has been rendered in the annals of ornithology and natural history writing, into which poetry (never far from this bird) creeps. The nightingale's poetic life then becomes the main focus of chapters Two and Three, which follow the nightingale's bewildering literary life, while Chapter Four explores how musical works are underpinned by a necessarily different, more direct, relationship with the nightingale's song. The focus of the final chapter is the nightingale's decline on British soil, and how this reflects back on the bird's cultural history, with an ear to the bird's disappearance. For 'Fled is that music,' writes Keats, and loss has long been written into what this bird means.[31]

F.N. fec.

1 Natural History Nightingales: 'When the Buds of the Leaves Are Swelling'

Nightingales are part of the Old World subfamily of chats (*Saxicolinae*). The nightingale, along with other chats, was formerly considered to be a member of the thrush family (*Turdidae*), but is now classed as of the Old World flycatcher family (*Muscicapidae*), in which sits the subfamily of robins and chats.[1] While chats may be closer genetically to Old World flycatchers, their morphological and behavioural similarities to thrushes suggest a common ancestry.

There are two species of nightingale. The common nightingale breeds in Western and Central Europe, the Middle East, northwestern Africa, the Caucasus and southern Russia, as well as east to southwestern Mongolia. The thrush nightingale replaces the common nightingale east of a line running from southern Denmark, northern Germany, southern Poland and through Eastern Europe to the western shores of the Black Sea. Where the two birds overlap, in Eastern Europe and southern Russia, the common and thrush nightingales sometimes hybridize. There are three races of common nightingale, although the differences between them are very slight: the *Luscinia megarhynchos megarhynchos*, the 'nominate' bird, is the most westerly, replaced in central Turkey by the *Luscinia megarhynchos africana*, while the eastern bird is *Luscinia megarhynchos golzii*. The European breeding population of the common nightingale is estimated at between 10.7 million

Common and thrush nightingales in Johann Andreas Naumann, *Naturgeschichte der Vögel Deutschlands* (1820–60).

and 20.3 million, and there are up to 500,000–800,000 pairs in France alone, while there are almost 6 million in Spain (which hosts 37 per cent of the European population).[2] The UK hosts between 2,400 and 3,900 pairs. We might compare the films *Jean de Florette* (dir. Claude Berri, 1986), in which the abundant nightingales of Provence provide the soundtrack, unnoticed, while in *The Triple Echo* (dir. Michael Apted, 1972), filmed in Wiltshire, a single nightingale is carefully remarked upon in the opening scene (the film is based on a novella by nightingale-lover and Kent dweller H. E. Bates). There are between 11 million and 20 million thrush nightingales in Europe. Both the thrush and common nightingale winter in sub-Saharan Africa. The common nightingale winters from Mauritania, southeast through Nigeria, to Ethiopia and Uganda, while the thrush nightingale inhabits a more southerly band from Tanzania, through Zimbabwe and Botswana, to the tip of South Africa.

In the UK, the nightingale's stronghold breeding grounds are mostly southeast of a line drawn from the Wash to Exeter, with the highest numbers in the southeastern counties of Essex, Suffolk, Norfolk, Kent and Sussex. At the start of the twentieth century, the birds were numerous over much of southern England below this nightingale line, and along the northwestern fringe, from Devon through the West Midlands to east Yorkshire, they were present but much less numerous.[3] Earlier works of natural history reveal a more extensive distribution of the bird in the North of England. Nightingales were once numerous in Yorkshire, and especially plentiful about Doncaster according to Thomas Pennant, writing in 1768. There was a minor contraction in the 1930s, although the nightingale population extended in Devon, yet by 1976 a major contraction was underway, and the population continues to shrink to a southeastern pocket.

Eastern nightingale, Kuwait.

The earliest record of the common nightingale in the UK is in Devon, from the end of the last glaciation, when the return of trees and broad-leaved forests to Britain brought about our woodland birds. Fossils suggest that nightingales arrived in Britain about 10,000 years ago. Once year-round African residents, as the ice retreated from Europe, and African temperatures increased, it seems likely that the nightingale began its migratory habit. It is thought that the distinction between the common and thrush nightingale was caused by geographical isolation during the last glacial period. The first record of the thrush nightingale in the UK is from 1911 in Fair Isle, and there were only three accepted reports before 1965, all on that island. The first record in England was at Low Hauxley, Northumberland, in September 1965. Records of thrush nightingale sightings have increased since then, reflecting the extension of the bird's breeding range north and west. By 2015, 208 birds had been recorded in the UK. The eastern race *golzii* has been recorded twice in England – on the Isles of Scilly in 1987 and in Yorkshire in 1991.

The nightingale's colourings span a spectrum of brown to white: a warm milk-chocolate brown above, with brighter russet-brown edges to the wings, rump and tail. Its buff-white underside is washed with sandy light brown to breast and flanks, while the throat is paler. The bird's large black eyes are bordered by pale eye-rings, and it is often said to have a gentle expression. At 15–17 cm (6–7 in.), and weighing around 20 g (0.7 oz), the nightingale is slightly larger than a robin (it has a smaller head but a longer tail). The male is marginally bigger, but the sexes are otherwise alike. The juvenile is similar to the adult, although slightly duller or darker brown, with a more speckled appearance, spotted brown on the upperparts with scaling on the throat and lower flanks.

The nightingale is notoriously secretive and skulks – although less so on mainland Europe – tending to keep low, undercover and just above or on ground, making it difficult to locate. It flies at low level, no more than is essential, at short distances. The bird usually sings from deep within bushy and densely vegetated habitats,

Eastern nightingale, Kuwait.

36

although it does venture out to sing from a branch or even rooftop (behaviour which is more widely reported, even common, in France and Spain, where the bird is known to be less shy). Its movements are similar to that of a robin, although less rapid, hopping and running alertly on long legs. The thrush nightingale is difficult to distinguish from the common nightingale. Generally, it is drabber or greyer, and less rufous in its colouring. Its chest and flanks are a mottled, dusky brown, and on well-marked birds the chest may be completely suffused brown. The wings of the thrush nightingale are also more pointed than that of a robin, and it has a marginally longer tail.

The oldest reported ringed nightingale was seven years and eleven months old, although the eighteenth-century French naturalist Georges-Louis Leclerc, Comte de Buffon, claimed that he knew a nightingale that reached the age of seventeen, growing grey and then white, and remarked that the bird never paired: 'love seemed to abridge the period of life'.[4]

Thrush nightingale, Uglich, Russia.

The nightingale's song tends to begin with a series of pure, rising, flute-like notes, before a loaded pause yields to a diverse series of phrases – rich, bubbling notes, long and short, whistles, trills, high and low, purrs, rattles, gurgles, rapid machine gunfire – separated by further pauses and marked by a loud whistling crescendo, usually rounded off with a flourish or sudden sharp note, before it all begins again. The song of the thrush nightingale is less varied: it is slower, with longer pauses between phrases. This song lacks the celebrated crescendo of the common nightingale, and is often described as drier and more mechanical, with scratchier, rattling notes and phrases.

The daytime song of the thrush nightingale is thought to be generally related to marking and defending territory, the nighttime song to attracting the female birds (paired birds sing during the night too, however). During the day, males sing from different locations within the breeding territory, in contrast to the nocturnal song, which tends to be delivered from the same place for consecutive nights. The daytime song is usually shorter and more repetitious, with less variety. The bird sings with its head held up and bill open, orange gape revealed, its body vibrating and trembling with sound. The sound of the nightingale's song declines through May, as pairs are formed and the young are hatched: it is mostly over by the first week of June.

Because the nightingale has long been famed as the foremost singer of the natural world, its song the gold standard of birdsong, other admired songbirds have been honoured with the epithet of 'nightingale' even when the species has been absent. The blackcap is the northern nightingale, the sedge warbler the Irish or Scotch nightingale, and the robin the winter nightingale. In the United States, the northern cardinal is known as the Virginia nightingale; in Sweden, the bluethroat is the nightingale of the mountains;

Persian nightingale by J. G. Keulemans, in H. E. Dresser, *A History of the Birds of Europe*, vol. I (1871–81).

while the northern mockingbird is known simply as the nightingale in Jamaica. Among humans, there are countless applications for the epithet, from medieval Persian poet Hafiz – the nightingale of Shiraz – to Edith Piaf, Jean Cocteau's 'nightingale of France'.

Nightingale song is loud and commands attention. In Berlin, where nightingales sing next to busy roads, its volume rises to 93 decibels, louder than a train whistle. Many onomatopoeic sounds have been ascribed to the bird's song. The Greek nightingale sings 'itu, itu', a reference to Itys, from the myth of Philomela, while in English literary tradition the main syllable is 'jug', immortalized by Coleridge's 'murmurs musical and swift jug jug', and corrupted in the twentieth century to T. S. Eliot's '"jug jug" to dirty ears'.[5] Other associated sounds include 'tiotinx', 'wine', 'tara-dei' and 'oci', yet it can be difficult to tell whether these sounds are heard in the nightingale's song or derived from its lore (more on this in the next chapter), as in the Greek syllabling of 'itu', or the French 'oci' (kill). Naturalist and documentary-maker Oliver Pike spent a season observing nightingales in an Oxfordshire wood in the 1920s, and recorded this time in his 1932 book *The Nightingale: Its Story and Song*, in which he tells of hearing a nightingale call 'jug-jug' forty times in succession. He writes that 'the chief charm' of the bird's song, however, 'is a beautiful, long-drawn whistle, a very pure note', which the majority of birds are shy of uttering: alas, 'no written words could give any idea of the beauty of these [notes]'.[6] Researchers at the Free University of Berlin – home to long-term research and a huge range of studies on nightingale song – recently identified the penchant of the male nightingale to insert an unusual 'buzz' in its song, which they evidenced is the sound most popular with female nightingales (behavioural activities of female birds listening to a playback of the sound were used as measures of arousal).[7] It is thought to be a difficult sound for the bird to make, requiring skilled control of

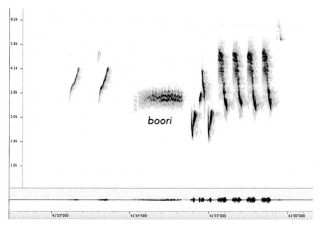

boori

Sonogram showing the nightingale 'boori' sound.

the syrinx (the bird equivalent of the larynx) and thus indicative of a good, strong choice for mating. Musician and philosopher David Rothenberg has called this the 'boori' sound, 'the sexiest of all nightingale tones'.[8] He writes, 'think of that one fuzzy sound as a buzz, whirr, scratch, hook, or riff that stands out from the other sounds. *Brrrrrrrrjjrrrrrhh!*'[9] Rothenberg also reminds us that the nightingale's song is 'an extreme example of what evolution can produce through sexual selection, as generations of female birds have preferred increasingly refined and nuanced songs', and evidence of Charles Darwin's theory that birds have a 'natural aesthetic sense'.[10] Not loaned from heaven, or an echo of the music of the spheres, the power of the nightingale's song lies in the process of female choice and mating signals. Further unpoetic explanation for the vigour of the nightingale's song has emerged from recent research at the University of Bath and Cornell University, where it has been found that the complexity of nightingale song maps onto their brain structure, with the region of the birds' brain responsible for song being larger in nightingales in comparison with other songbirds.

Nightingales arrive in breeding territories in mid- to late April in the UK (earlier in Spain and other warmer countries), having departed from wintering grounds in mid- to late March. The thrush nightingale arrives later to some territories: in Sweden and western Russia in late April and early May, and in central Russia and northern Kazakhstan later in May. The males arrive about a week prior to the females, usually returning to traditional nesting sites, and begin their celebrated song once territory is established. As with most bird species, dispersal distance from natal to breeding territory is greater for females than males.

Pairs form for the duration of the breeding season, and only a small number re-form in subsequent years. Pike was particularly taken with the nightingale's courtship ritual:

Nightingale, *Luscinia megarhynchos*, illustration of 1596–1610 by Anselmus Boëtius de Boodt.

We have seen him bowing before her, opening and spreading his fine tail, fluttering his wings, and really performing what I can only call a waltz. He sits on a branch close to her, and during the whole time is moving, not rapidly, but in a most graceful manner . . . I have never watched a more beautiful display by any bird.[11]

The ritual can be seen in Pike's nightingale instalment in the *Secrets of Nature* series of documentary films of 1932.

Scrub is the nightingale's original and preferred habitat, but the bird breeds in a variety of wooded habitats with rich undergrowth. In England, both its woodland and scrub territories have in common extremely dense, almost-impenetrable thickets of vegetation within 2 m (6½ ft) of the ground. Both of these habitats are dynamic, however, and conditions remain suitable for nightingales for a limited period of time. British Trust for Ornithology (BTO) guidance shows that the ideal formation of scrub for nightingales is vigorous thickets with a dense canopy of twigs and leaves, shading out the plants below and leaving the ground free from vegetation, but with a covering of leaf litter.[12] The best patches contain blackthorn, hawthorn and, on wetter sites, willow, yet the structure of the scrub – the dense canopy – is more important than species. This ideal structure, surrounded by a thick field layer of brambles, rank grass or nettles, typically occurs in pioneering scrub, which colonizes open land.[13] In the 1970s, surveys conducted in the UK found that around a quarter of nightingale territories were located in scrub, which rose to half in the most recent BTO survey (2012). The nightingale nests in birch and hazel woodlands in Northern and Central Europe (coppiced areas cut every twelve to fifteen years), as well as oak and beech woods with fallen trees, hedgerows, thickets, overgrown parks, large gardens and orchards, provided there are hedges or bushy areas,

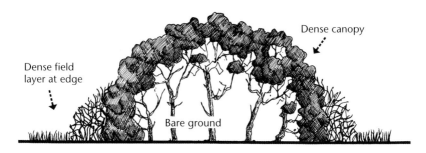

Dense canopy

Dense field
layer at edge

Bare ground

British Trust for
Ornithology
cross-section of
ideal nightingale
scrub breeding
habitat.

with hawthorn or other thorn scrub.[14] Both common and thrush nightingales like damp areas of riparian thickets or overgrown woods near water, although this is almost the sole type of habitat favoured by the thrush nightingale. Only the common nightingale can be found in much drier and warmer breeding territories such as the hillsides of the Mediterranean. It has often been said that nightingales are fond of the vicinity of an echo. In places where the nightingale is more abundant, the birds nest closer to human settlements and may even sing from rooftops. In Belgium, the Netherlands and southern France, the common nightingale can be found in bushy coastal sand dunes, while in Berlin the bird has returned to the city-centre parks. It has long been a mainstay of city parks in Armenia. Climate determines the bird's breeding range, restricting nightingales to places in which the mean July temperature sits between 17 and 30°C (between 62 and 86°F). In Europe, the bird breeds mostly below 1,000 m (3,280 ft) – in Britain rarely above 200 m (670 ft) – whereas in Central Asia it nests in areas up to 2,600 m (8,530 ft).[15]

Paired nightingales begin nesting in May. The site is chosen by the female bird, who also builds the nest, which is well concealed in thick undergrowth on or near the ground. The nest is made of dead leaves, dry grasses, feathers and animal hair. Eggs typically number four to five and are pale olive-green-blue with reddish-brown speckles or spots, and hatch after thirteen to fourteen days. Initially, the young are fed solely by the mother, with food brought to the nest by the father. As the chicks grow, however, both parents forage to keep up with demand. Pike's nightingale documentary includes impressive footage of the parents feeding their young, imagined as 'true Oliver Twists,

Nightingale nest and egg, from F. O. Morris, *A Natural History of the Nests and Eggs of British Birds* (1853–6).

always asking for more'. The young remain in the nest for ten to twelve days after they hatch: they are able to fly within five days of leaving and are able to forage for themselves within nine days. In warmer territories, common nightingale pairs often rear two broods in a season, whereas cold British summers limit the clutch to one (the colder environs of thrush nightingales also means that they rear one brood per season). The family stays together for about two weeks, and after the young have fledged, all venture further afield for richer feeding sites. The nightingale forages mainly on the ground, within and below undergrowth. Its diet includes earthworms, beetles, woodlice, grasshoppers, ants, moth larvae, ant pupae, flies, spiders and other invertebrates; berries and seeds are taken in late summer and autumn. In late June the adult birds begin actively moulting (the process of shedding and replacing worn-out feathers) in preparation for the flight back to Africa.

Birds typically depart from England in August and early September. The precise migration route and wintering locations of nightingales were, for a long time, something of a mystery, until

Fledgling common nightingale.

in July 2009 the BTO tracked a number of British nightingales using the latest geolocation technology. Some devices failed, but that of one bird, named OAD, had recorded the outward journey: the bird left the Cambridgeshire Fens and passed west of Paris in the second week of August, passing Madrid two weeks later on a journey to southern Portugal, where it remained from 1 to 19 September. It then crossed the Atlantic to the west coast of North Africa, and moved slowly south for the following six weeks. By mid-November it had stopped on the border of Senegambia, where it spent a month, before moving south through Guinea Bissau and arriving at its final wintering site in western Guinea in mid-December.[16] It is thought that most nightingales that come to England winter in the West African countries Sierra Leone, Guinea or Guinea-Bissau. The bird's wintering habitat is the thorny scrub and forest edges of savanna woodland, as well as bushes fringing rivers and other bodies of water, and sometimes tall grass. The nightingale gives a more subdued or less rich version of its song, intermittently: it's not known exactly why – possibly as sub-song (a rehearsal for spring) or for holding territory. The song increases in frequency towards spring, and the bird also sings on passage. Birds depart wintering areas from mid-March after feeding, having built up fat stores to see them cover a huge distance around the Sahara. One tagged nightingale, after departing from Sierra Leone, took just three days to travel – without stopping – all the way to Portugal, taking a coastal route. British birds tend to take a break for food and rest in southern Portugal and Spain before leaving for England in mid-April.[17]

Nightingales feature in natural history's earliest works. While the details of migration were not understood until much later, it has always been known that the birds arrive and breed in the spring: both Aristotle and Pliny wrote that nightingales sing continuously day and night for fifteen days – presumably the intense

Adult nightingale, *Luscinia megarhynchos*, at nest with chicks.

period of song when the birds first arrive – 'when the buds of the leaves are swelling'.[18] As noted in the Introduction, the nightingale as a bird of spring is one of the few accurate associations that runs across natural history, poetry and lore, from their earliest days.

Other aspects of nightingale misapprehension are rooted in the classical period. In his *History of Animals*, composed in the fourth century BC, Aristotle mistakenly notes that both the male and female bird sing. Pliny's singing nightingale is also female, and he notes that the mother birds teach the young to sing. (He did have it right that nightingales – like all songbirds – acquire their music, yet it is from listening to their fathers.) Pliny's celebrated description of the nightingale's song was quoted in many early works of ornithology. This, together with Philomela's mythological transformation into the bird, fuelled belief in the idea of the female as singer. In what is often considered the first work of systematic ornithology in England, *The Ornithology of Francis Willoughby* (1678, first published in Latin in 1676 and completed by John Ray after Willoughby's death), the nightingale, 'chief of all singing birds', is again depicted as female, and Willoughby draws on Pliny to praise 'her admirable skill in singing, her study and contention, the sweetness of her accents, the great variety of her notes, the harmonious modulation and inflection of her voice'.[19]

Modern readers might be surprised by the poeticism of early ornithological writing: in his *Natural History* (first published in French as *Histoire naturelle* in 36 volumes from 1749 to 1804), the Comte de Buffon, for example, readily hymns the experience of hearing the nightingale sing on

> soft warm evenings in spring, when the air is still and serene, and all nature seems to listen to the songster of the grove . . . the soft breaths of love and joy are poured from his inmost soul, and every heart beats unison, and melts with delicious languor.[20]

Naturalist writings also drew directly on poems as sources of ornithological knowledge and judgement. In his popular work *British Zoology* (1768), as well as quoting Pliny, Thomas Pennant includes a number of quotations from poems by John Milton in his section on the nightingale. He observes that 'This was the favourite bird of the British poet, who omits no opportunity of introducing it . . . These quotations from the best judge of melody we thought due to the sweetest of our feathered choristers.'[21]

In nearly all of these quotations, the singing bird is female, melancholy and heard singing only at night, yet Pennant lets these stand as the nightingale's truth. Indeed, he prefaces the famous quotation from Pliny with the observation that he only 'in general' expresses 'the truth'. A more accurate and scientific strand of ornithology did emerge in the nineteenth century, however. In an entry on the nightingale in his *Ornithological Dictionary* (1802), George Montagu notes that 'we confine our pen to the facts of natural history . . . we must refer our readers to the *British Zoology*, for the more classical and elegant information,' as elegance gives way to 'facts'.[22] Montagu clarifies in his work that it is the male bird that sings to attract a mate, the first – at least in British ornithology – to assert this (although he was pre-empted by Coleridge's 'The Nightingale', which had the bird as male four years earlier). Similarly, in his *Birds of Europe* (1837), John Gould preferred to confine his section on the nightingale to 'details connected with it habits and the localities it prefers', rather than 'the merits of its vocal powers or to indulging in strains of useless admiration'.[23]

Some naturalists did seek to prove the merits of the nightingale's song scientifically, however. In his 'Essay on the Language of Birds' (1773), Daines Barrington sets out 'experiments and observations . . . related to the singing of birds, which is a subject that hath never been scientifically treated of', and attempts to affix 'precise ideas' to the nightingale's celebrated descriptions.[24] Having recruited the anatomist John Hunter to dissect a number of birds in order to examine their vocal chords, Barrington found the muscles of the 'larynx' to be stronger in the nightingale than in any bird of the same size (this is reflected in more recent research on nightingale brain size and structure). He also observed the variety in the nightingale's song, noting sixteen different beginnings and closes in one song cycle, and attempted to take down some passages according to musical intervals. He found not only this to be impossible but that the bird's song 'eludes all verbal description'.[25] The results he did glean were used to create a table 'by which the comparative merit of the British singing birds may be examined'.[26] The nightingale clearly wins, scoring nineteen out of twenty for 'compass' and 'execution' and in a turn aside from the poetical, Barrington, in a supposedly scientific manner, deems the nightingale's song to be superlative. He also deduced that its song was 'plaintive', for which it also scored

Nightingale cock, hen and egg, in Eleazar Albin, *A Natural History of English Songbirds* (1737).

50

Nightingale, Cock, Hen, and Egg.

nineteen, higher than any other bird (although it did also score fourteen for 'sprightly').

One of the more curious observations made in early works of ornithology is the phenomenon of talking nightingales. In his *Natural History*, Pliny tells of how the sons of Emperor Claudius owned nightingales that spoke Greek and Latin, and there was a particularly popular account of talking birds in Conrad Gesner's *History of Animals* of 1555, reproduced in many subsequent works. The tale goes that a correspondent of Gesner's staying at an inn at Ratisbon (present-day Regensburg) in 1546, couldn't sleep one night and discovered caged nightingales 'talking with one another, and plainly imitating men[']s discourses', repeating what they had heard during the day.[27] This included an argument between the house servant and his wife, which included many 'filthy' and 'immodest' words, and a prediction of the imminent war of

Daines Barrington, 'table, by which the comparative merit of the British singing birds may be examined', in 'Experiments and Observations on the Singing of Birds', *Proceedings of the Royal Society of London, Philosophical Transactions of the Royal Society* (1773).

	Mellowness of tone.	Sprightly notes.	Plaintive notes.	Compass.	Execution.
Nightingale	19	14	19	19	19
Skylark	4	19	4	18	18
Woodlark	18	4	17	12	8
Titlark	12	12	12	12	12
Linnet	12	16	12	16	18
Goldfinch	4	19	4	12	12
Chaffinch	4	12	4	8	8
Greenfinch	4	4	4	4	6
Hedge-sparrow . . .	6	0	6	4	4
Aberdavine (or Siskin) .	2	4	0	4	4
Redpoll	0	4	0	4	4
Thrush	4	4	4	4	4
Blackbird	4	4	0	2	2
Robin	6	16	12	12	12
Wren	0	12	0	4	4
Reed-sparrow	0	4	0	2	2
Black-cap, or the Norfolk Mock nightingale [k] .	14	12	12	14	14

the emperor against the Protestants. Readers and ornithologists readily believed the astonishing tale.

Much early ornithological knowledge came from manuals and guides on keeping caged birds. Songbirds were kept for entertainment from the time of Aristotle, and nightingales were the most popular due to their song. In Pliny's day, they could fetch more money than a person sold as a slave. Information on the breeding cycle, habitat and habits of these birds was needed to catch and then keep them alive. Feeding this insectivore bird was a challenge. In his lavish handbook of caged-bird care, *Uccelliera* (1622), Giovanni Pietro Olina provided a detailed pasta recipe, comprised of chickpea flour, almonds, butter and egg yolks. Olina also gives advice on encouraging the nightingale to sing. He recommends a musical concert, which is 'infinitely effective' due to the 'Sympathy that this little Bird has with SYMPHONY and music', and also observes that the nightingale is particularly good at picking out scents, and that placing herbs in the cage will stimulate the bird to sing.[28] Olina made important observations on nightingales and territory (although he borrowed extensively from his predecessor Antonio Valli da Todi), noting that the male bird takes up a '*franchise* or *freehold*, into which it does not admit any other Nightingales save only its FEMALE PARTNER'.[29]

Another important discovery was made through caged birds. In his anonymously published treatise on nightingales, *Traité du rossignol* (1697), the physician Nicolas Venette made the discovery of migratory restlessness (usually referred to by the German term *Zugunruhe*).[30] Venette noticed that in February and March, or mid-September, caged nightingales became impatient, flying and struggling against the bars of their cages, and 'it is this instinct and inner guide that makes them fly with a favourable wind directly to the place where they want to go'.[31] This instinct was so

Making pasta for nightingales, Giovanni Pietro Olina's handbook of caged-bird care, *Uccelliera* (1622).

Prompting nightingales to sing with music, from *Uccelliera* (1622).

strong that the wings of caged nightingales had to be tied down to prevent them from beating themselves to death.

Ornithological discourse more widely was undecided on migration until well into the nineteenth century, one of the few aspects of the nightingale on which commentators more openly expressed uncertainty. Willoughby observed that the nightingale was 'very impatient of cold, and therefore in Winter-time either hides itself in some lurking place, or flies away into hot countries'.[32] The poet and natural historian Charlotte Smith remarked in her *Natural History of Birds* (1807) that 'doubts have arisen, whether the Nightingales really depart with departing summer', for they had not been seen at sea, like other birds, and 'may find in woods and coppices the larvae of insects enough to support their existence during winter'.[33] (The subject fascinates Gilbert White in relation to his favourite species, the swallow, which is, of course, much discussed in his *Natural History of Selborne* of

1789.) Smith had written this ambiguity into an earlier poem, sonnet VII, 'On the Departure of the Nightingale':

Whether on Spring thy wandering flights await,
Or whether silent in our groves you dwell
The pensive muse shall own thee for her mate.[34]

Whatever the facts, ornithological knowledge here is in balance with poetry in its uncertainty.

In his *Natural History of Cage Birds* (1795), Johann Matthäus Bechstein remarked on the nightingale's character: 'he has a serious circumspect air, but his foresight is not proportioned to it, for he falls readily into all the snares which are laid for him.'[35] He notes that the birds are known for being 'silly and curious', and 'nothing is easier than to catch a nightingale in the season of spring'.[36] According to eighteenth-century bird fanciers, there were three species of nightingale – the mountain nightingale, the field nightingale and the water nightingale.[37] The *Annual Register* for 1764 reported that a man in London was able to attract nightingales by his song, they alighted on him, and were caught by his hand. In his *Birds of Middlesex* (1866), James Harting reports that a friend of his, an expert in bird-catching, caught fifteen-dozen nightingales in a good season, and received 18 shillings per dozen for them in London. On one occasion, he caught nineteen before breakfast. Most birds did not survive in captivity. John Gould noted that at least nine out of ten die within a month of their capture. Among birds that did survive – usually those that had not mated – caged nightingales sung for a much longer period than those in the wild. William Yarrell writes that a male may be kept in song for three months, and knew of one bird that had sung for 114 successive days.

The range of the nightingale in the UK has perplexed natural historians, especially the bird's absence in the mild woodlands of

Devonshire and Cornwall. One theory was that the nightingale was only found where cowslips grew plentifully – a flower that was also thought to be absent in the southwest. Explanations for the bird's unexpected, localized absence came in the form of a prayer by Edward the Confessor, who, annoyed by the songs which interrupted his devotions, prayed that nightingales might never be heard at Havering-atte-Bower in Essex, and, since a hermit cursed nightingales at St Leonard's Forest near Worth in Sussex, they never returned to the area. Attempts have been made to extend the nightingales' distribution. Yarrell remembers how

Birds of Great Britain and Ireland by Arthur G. Butler, with illustrations by Henrik Grönvold and Frederick William Frohawk (1907–8).

A gentleman of Gower . . . procured from Norfolk and Surrey, a few years back, some scores of young Nightingales, hoping that an acquaintance with his beautiful woods and their mild climate would induce a second visit; but the law of Nature was too strong for him, and not a single bird returned.[38]

A similar attempt was made in Scotland by Sir John Sinclair (1754–1835), who purchased a number of nightingale eggs from a London bird-catcher and employed several men to place the eggs in the nest of robins in Caithness. The birds were successfully reared by the foster parents, yet did not return the following breeding season. In 1891 Eugene Schieffelin attempted to introduce nightingales to North America. Schieffelin was a member of the American Acclimatization Society that sought to introduce European plants and animals to U.S. soil, and the nightingale was one of forty bird species mentioned in Shakespeare's plays that Schieffelin took across the Atlantic in homage to his literary hero, in a curious new twist in the weave of nature–culture relations. While the nightingale was one of the scheme's failures, the 32 starlings he released into New York City's Central Park in 1890 have now become 200 million disruptive birds in North America today.

The bird's fame also drew American nature writers to the UK in search of the Old World species. John Burroughs described his 'hunt for the nightingale' – an important English countryside delight he was determined to experience – in *Fresh Fields* (1887). Burroughs undertakes his mission in late June and is almost thwarted by his timing at the very end of nightingale season, yet he does manage to hear a few bars of the bird's song. It is enough to satisfy Burroughs that 'here is the complete artist, of whom all the other birds are but hints and studies', describing the song as

Common
nightingale,
Pulborough
Brooks, Sussex.

'bright, startling, assured, of great compass and power'.[39] 'None
but the nightingale could have inspired Keats's ode.'[40]

Burroughs's comment brings us back to the place of the nightingale's literary history in its natural history. While some works
may have tried to separate the two, the power of the nightingale's
poetic life has defied such a separation. In her *Natural History of
Birds*, in addition to ornithological details, Charlotte Smith is concerned with how the 'Nightingale is the most known and admired
of all the songsters, and is celebrated by the poets more than any
other of the feathered race'. This almost becomes the bird's most
salient feature, and she includes quotations from a number of
poems.[41] The poems are not there to provide information and
judgement, as in Pennant, but are a fundamental part of the bird's

identity. While other species such as the cuckoo, robin and skylark may have rich cultural lives, the force of the nightingale's cultural history within its natural history is unique. More recently, in the Poyser Country Avifauna *Birds in England* (2005), across 550 species and 694 pages, only in the nightingale section does poetry appear, an excerpt from Milton's *Paradise Lost*. In the *Collins Bird Guide* – first published in 1999, with a second edition released in 2010 – only the nightingale has its cultural fame acknowledged. The same is true for the latest of hard-bitten ornithological identification guides, *Robins and Chats* (2015). These are works quite separate from the 'new nature writing', which often explores poetry alongside the ecology and science. For the nightingale, poetry is part of the bird's truth, its 'jizz' (the term used by birders to describe the overall impression of a bird).

2 Literary Nightingales: 'Old-World Pain'

The nightingale's song has meant many things to those who have written about it: love, spring, sex, death, joy. Its deepest association, however, is with what the Victorian poet Matthew Arnold described as 'that wild, unquench'd, deep-sunken, old-world pain' (an emotional matching with the bird's distribution), which goes right back to the origins of the nightingale's literary history in the classical period.[1] This chapter follows the vast, largely poetic literary history of the nightingale from its melancholy origins in the classical period to its apex of joy in the Romantic period, and the vacillations of emotion and experience that the bird has evoked in the intervening centuries. As frequently as the nightingale has been invoked as muse or symbol of the poet, this has affected how it has been depicted – often at the cost of closer observation and accuracy. Yet, throughout its literary history, the bird is always poised somewhere between 'real' bird, in its natural habitat, and literary symbol, the balance between the two ever shifting.

The earliest known poetic passage on the nightingale is in Homer's epic poem the *Odyssey* (composed *c.* 675–725 BC): in book XIX, Penelope, wife of absent Odysseus, speaks of the qualities her sorrow takes on with the night:

Nightingale, from *The Poetry of Birds, selected from various authors; with coloured illustrations. By a Lady* (1833).

> After the night comes and sleep has taken all others,
> I lie on my bed, and the sharp anxieties swarming

61

Thick and fast on my beating heart torment my
    sorrowing self.
As when Pandereos' daughter, the greenwood
    nightingale,
perching in the deep of the forest foliage sings out
her lovely song, when springtime has just begun; she,
    varying
the manifold strains of her voice, pours out the melody,
    mourning
Itylos, son of the lord Zethos, her own beloved
Child, whom she once killed with the bronze when the
    madness was on her;
So my mind is divided and starts one way, then another.[2]

It's a strange simile, not positing a straightforward analogy through grief, but rather making a connection between the quality of the bird's night-time song and the machinations of her anxious mind: the variety and changeability so often celebrated in the

Nightingale in
song, Sussex.

nightingale's song, 'start[ing] one way, then another'. Penelope here refers to the myth of Aedon, daughter of Pandareus, who accidentally kills her son Itylus instead of her intended victim: one of the children of Niobe (Aedon envied her greater number of off-spring). So fierce was Aedon's grief that the gods changed her into a nightingale. The tale is closely related to the Philomela myth, and the bird here sings its most stubborn mythological meaning of grief, albeit from 'deep' within its natural habitat.

The appropriation of the nightingale is usually about expression and inspiration rather than psychological processes, and the bird, 'Russet-coated, / Vibrant-throated', is first cast as 'woodland muse' in Aristophanes' comedy *The Birds* (414 BC), invoked by the chorus:

> Chief musician of the woodland,
> Sweetly fluting,
> Spring-saluting,
> Seldom seen though often heard.
> . . .
> Come, woodland Muse,
> Tio, tio, tio, tiotinx,
> With changeful melodies inspire me as of old,
> Tio, tio, tio, tiotinx.[3]

The bird's song is represented by the sound of the flute in the play, yet it also inspires and underscores the play's poetic language more widely. Aristophanes here presents what is perhaps the earliest of attempts to represent birdsong in language, explored through syllabling sounds – 'tio tio tio' – and experiments with form, varying the rhythms and lengths of lines.

Melancholy, expressiveness and the poet come together in Virgil's *Georgics* (29 BC). In book IV, celebrated poet of myth

Orpheus mourns the loss of his wife, Eurydice; his lament is likened
to that of the nightingale, as, slumped on the banks of the Strymon,
he sings a 'broken-hearted threnody':[4]

> Just as a nightingale will sorrow under poplar shade
> for her lost brood which some brute ploughboy spotted
> and pilfered from the nest, though it was not yet fledged.
> That bird still weeps by night and, perched in a tree,
>   repeats
> her plaintive keen, filling far and wide with the ache of her
>   heartbreak.[5]

The nightingale mourns the loss of offspring, but there's no
explicit reference to the lament of Philomela or Aedon. This is a
nightingale in its natural habitat (*Georgics* – an agricultural poem
– is, by nature, a more naturalistic work), victim to human brut-
ishness, its powerful song reaching far and wide, yet plaintive
still.

Swimming in and around these works, then, is of course the
Philomela myth, formalized by Ovid in AD 8. The theme of Ovid's

Metamorphoses is the transformations of form, whereby the stories that play out in the mythic arena account for natural phenomena. The particularly violent tale of Philomela (or Philomele) and Procne is found in book VI. The two sisters are the daughters of Pandion, a legendary king of Athens. Procne marries Tereus, the king of Thrace, in an ill-omened union, which produces a son, Itys. Five years pass, and Procne grows anxious to see her sister, whence Tereus sails to Athens to fetch her. As soon as Tereus sets eyes on Philomela, he is overcome with a violent desire for her and, back in Thrace, he drags Philomela to a cabin in the woods, rapes her and cuts out her tongue to prevent her from telling her tale. Tereus tells Procne that Philomela is dead. A year passes with Philomela imprisoned in the cabin, when she notices a loom, uses it to weave her tale into fabric and sends it to Procne. One day, during the festival of Bacchus, Procne fetches Philomela from the cabin and takes her back to the palace. They kill Itys out of revenge and cook and serve him in a stew to Tereus. Philomela rushes in with Itys' head and flings it at Tereus who, in rage, grief and disgust, draws out his sword and pursues the two sisters:

As they flee,
You'd think they float on wings. Yes, sure enough,
They float on wings! One daughter seeks the woods,
One rises to the roof; and even now
The marks of murder show up a breast
And feathers carry still the stamp of blood.
And he, grief-spurred, swift-swooping for revenge,
Is changed into a bird that bears a crest,
With, for a sword, a long fantastic bill –
A hoopoe, every inch a fighter still.[6]

Here is the very moment of metamorphosis, in which the lines
of Ovid's poem seem almost implicated: one moment the sisters
seem to float on wings, the next they do so, propelled by the author's
imaginings. In earlier Greek versions (which particularly suggest
links with the Aedon myth), Philomela was the swallow and Procne
the nightingale, whereas in Latin works the identities are reversed.
Interestingly, Ovid is neutral on the topic, and does not specify
which is which – nor does he identify the species beyond the clues
of location – but translators, and Ovid's poetic successors, have
insisted on Philomela as the nightingale, forever singing her sor-
rowful tale. The association is already suggested in the location of
her rape and imprisonment – hidden away among 'dark ancient
trees' in the forest. The myth has had enormous cultural value,
fuelled by the popularity of Ovid, among the favourite poets of
Chaucer and Shakespeare, who both draw on the Philomela myth
in their works. By the twenty-first century, in Margaret Atwood's
version of the myth, the nightingale sings, but the 'story of the
story of the story' and the myth continues to have wide cultural
influence: the recent film *The Nightingale* (dir. Jennifer Kent, 2018)
is a horrific rape-revenge drama in which the victim is nicknamed
the nightingale due to her beautiful singing voice.[7]

Philomela
and Procne,
in *A Hundred
Fables of
La Fontaine*,
illustrations
by Percy
J. Billinghurst
(1900).

66

PHILOMEL ·AND· PROGNE.

How does the Philomela story function as a myth? The hoopoe's bill is explained by Tereus' sword, while the suggestion is that the feathers of swallow and nightingale 'carry still the stamp of blood', accounting for the russet shades of the nightingale and red throat of the swallow. In his *History of Animals* (350 BC), Aristotle observes that the nightingale has a truncated tongue, which, later in the eighteenth century, Buffon speculated could have given rise to the Philomela myth. No mention is made of the nightingale's song in Ovid, yet the myth is rooted in themes of silencing and expression. Following the violent loss of her tongue, Philomela first 'speaks' through the tapestry she creates, before finding a new voice through her metamorphosis. The nightingale's association with lament was also already well established. In *Phaedo* (360 BC), Plato represents Socrates as contradicting the notion that nightingale, swallow and hoopoe all sing in sorrow: no bird sings when it is hungry or cold or experiences some other such pain, he says. In his *Description of Greece* (second century AD), Pausanias contemplates the origins of the fable, the story of which is here a real-life event:

> The women went to Athens, and there, mourning both their wrongs and their revenge, they wept themselves to death. The fable that they were turned into a nightingale and a swallow was suggested, I suppose, by the plaintive and dirge-like song of these birds.[8]

History or myth, Greek or Roman, the cultural imagination seized on the nightingale as a melancholic singer.

After the classical period, the principal meaning of the nightingale's song became one of love – variously divine, earthly and bawdy. Philomela is used as a synonym for the bird, yet for a period all vestiges of the unhappy myth drop from it, and instead

A nightingale in its nest, from Jacob van Maerlant, *Der naturen bloeme* (c. 1350).

she suggests the renewal, joy and fecundity that come with the spring. While the bird's supposed melancholy is the most difficult of its meanings to account for, the association with love and spring maps more seamlessly onto the nightingale's natural history (although the differing refractions of love still belie the tendency of the poet to fill 'all things with himself', to make 'all gentle sounds tell back' their own tale).

In early Christian Latin poetry, praise of the nightingale's song and its invocation is steeped in divine love and praise. Bishop Paulinus of Nola (d. 431) asks God that he might be inspired to sing like the nightingale: 'Make me tuneful, with a sweet voice, just like the bird of spring, she who, hiding beneath the green leaves, is accustomed to delight the pathless fields with harmonious melodies, and to pour forth from a single throat many voices in changeful song.'[9]

Owing to its springtime arrival, the nightingale was also associated with Easter, welcomed as the harbinger of Christ, while elegiac resonances return in poems in which the bird is also associated with the Passion, such as 'Philomena' by John Pecham (*c.* 1225–1292). In Pecham's poem, the nightingale sings the story of mankind, and as the song reaches its height at noon, the hour of Christ's crucifixion, the bird dies. This may draw on the legend that the nightingale knows the time of its death, and pours out its song at the top of a tree before dying at midday.

Latin lyrics also speak to earthly as well as divine love, and there is no shortage of bawdy nightingale verse. The poet and editor Fleur Adcock has translated a twelfth-century work in which the nightingale takes 'cupid's part', and both inflames and sings of desire:

> She's love's announcer and town-crier;
> she lights the spark and stokes the fire;
> she swells the lover with desire,
> then boasts that he'll pursue it.[10]

The nightingale's hidden leafy glade habitat is ideal for lovemaking, and the bird encourages the 'heated blade / to pierce a girl who was a maid', while her wanton song drives such ladies to 'burn' for such activities.[11]

These themes evolve in the first poems of the nightingale to be written in the vernacular – the works of the French troubadours and trouvères, and German Minnesingers – which also develop the association between nightingale and poet, yet outside a religious context. The nightingale comes and goes from the foreground of these poems, half 'real' bird, half symbol. It sings in its natural habitat, and it is the bird of love and of the poet, either inciting him to compose or reminding him of his inability to do so. The singing nightingale is almost exclusively male in these lyrics, ornithologically correct, while facilitating the identification with a male poet and his erotic desire. Troubadour Bernard de

Ventadour (1135–1194), known as the 'nightingale poet', inter-weaves love, desire, joy, spring, birdsong and his own song in his nightingale verse:

> When the fresh grass and the leaf appears, and the flower buds on the branch, and when the nightingale lifts his voice high and clear and sings his song, I rejoice in him, I rejoice in the flower, and I rejoice in myself, but even more in my lady.[12]

It is not only the bird's secretive rural habitat and fecund season of song that often facilitate love but, of course, its realm of night. Marie de France's twelfth-century 'Laüstic' (Breton for 'nightingale') tells of two knights who live in neighbouring houses, separated by a high wall. The wife of one of the knights falls in love with her bachelor neighbour, yet the only contact they are able to have is at night, conversing at their respective windows. When challenged by her husband about her nightly activity, the lady responds:

> Anyone who does not hear the song of the nightingale knows none of the joys of this world. This is why I come and stand here. So sweet is the song I hear by night that it brings me great pleasure. I take such delight in it and desire it so much that I can get no sleep at all.[13]

The theme of death re-emerges as the jealous husband traps and kills the nightingale. Aware that she can never see her beloved again, the lady sends him the nightingale corpse, which the dis-tressed knight seals in a golden casket, studded with stones, and carries with him at all times: love's relic, emblematic of its loss. Two hundred years later, the suggestiveness of 'listening to the nightingale' was more pronounced and less innocent. In one of the tales of the *Decameron* by Giovanni Boccaccio (composed *c*. 1349–53), Caterina, in order to bypass the law of her parents and to be with her beloved Ricciardo, sleeps outside on her balcony, ostensibly to listen to the nightingale. Throughout the night, the couple take 'great pleasure' in each other, setting the 'nightingale a-trilling a great many times'.[14] The bird may even suggest the penis, for when her parents see the two lovers lying together in the morning they can see Caterina 'had caught and was still holding the nightingale'.[15]

Some of these meanings are reflected in *The Owl and the Nightingale* (*c*. 1200), a significant poem and one of the earliest substantial texts to be written in Middle English. At the time of writing, the poem is being brought to a new audience by Poet Laureate Simon Armitage, who is making a new translation to be published in October 2021. It is the first of a number of bird debate poems that feature the nightingale, taking the form of a frame narrative in which a first-person speaker reports an overheard debate between the nightingale and one of its traditional rivals (in later poems, these include thrush, cuckoo and merle (blackbird). In *The Owl and the Nightingale*, the birds represent two different attitudes to life – the owl, sober and pessimistic, associated with ill omen, and the merry and irreverent nightingale, the bird of love. The poem is a masterpiece in how natural history detail and cultural reference might interweave, and reveals both the contemporary status of nightingale knowledge and the bird's more symbolic meanings.

The poem confirms the nightingale's association with spring and joy, yet, to the owl, the bird's song is steeped in lechery, not love. Attention is drawn to the temporariness of the nightingale's song due to the breeding cycle (the male nightingale usually only stops singing once the chicks have hatched), as the bird is likened

Pice quasi pertice q̄ uba indiscrimīe uocis exprimāt ut lō
per ramos eūi pendule importuna garulitate sonantes ꝫ
ꝰ neqēut lingꝰ insmone explicare sonū tam hūane uocis ūi
cantur de q̄ congꝫ quidam aūr pica lax̄ certa dominū deuore
salutar. Sime no uideas eē negabis auem picus a pico sat̄u
suo nomen sūpsit eo q̄ auspicus utebatur. Siam senit hāc au
em quidam bƷe diumū illo indicio qual̄ māq̄ tiiꝫ arbore indi
ficatur. clā̄ ut quicq̄ diu tenere no ꝑ q̄n stati excidat
ubi illa msterit.

Lvcinia auis ūn nom̄ sūpsit q̄
cantu suo significare solꝫ surgen
tis exortū diei est lucenia ē H
pingit custos cū oua quodam
sinu corpus ꝫ gremio sout
isomnē louge noctis latex̄
cantilene suauitate solaꝫ
ut m̄ uidetur h̄ sūmma est e
mtencō quo possit no minu
dulcedub; modulꝫ qm̄ setu corp
oris animare setus ouaꝫ souie lxane

imitata tenus illa mult̄ ꝫ pudici intuissim mole lapide uua
chio trahens ut possit alumnū panis sius parūul no deesse no
cturno cantu mestu paupertatis mulcet affetū ꝫ quinus suam
diem lucime no possit imitari imitatur tū ea sedulitate pi
etatis.

Nightingale
and bats in the
*Northumberland
Bestiary*
(1250–60).

to the summer yokel: 'Once he's penetrated under the skirt, his love immediately expires. And your temper's just the same – as soon as you're sitting on your brood, you're deprived of all your airs.'[16]

The poem is unusual in the amount of accurate natural history knowledge contained therein, its anthropomorphism notwithstanding. Much is made of the nightingale's habitat, 'unsanitary' according to the owl, for, as he points out, it is near to where people go to the loo: 'it's next to the hedges and the thick weeds, where the thorns and twigs are tangled together, just where people go to do their business . . . You sit and sing behind the toilet-seat.'[17]

Reference is also made to the bird's absence from Ireland and Scotland, and its winter disappearance. The anonymous poet gives the impression that he is a close observer of the natural world, even as he becomes bewitched, like many before him, by the nightingale's song: 'She sang so loudly and so penetratingly that it was as if ringing harps were being played.'[18] There are no such hymns for the owl, and, as such, this praise implicitly wins the nightingale the debate, yet here the poet's bewitchment doesn't compromise accuracy. Interestingly, while the nightingale of the poem is a specific bird, it also speaks as every nightingale. It is the bird of all fable, as well as this bird, singing now. Bird of symbol and springtime scrub are one and the same; this poem does not differentiate and speaks to what a nightingale – across the sweep of nature and culture – 'is'.

One of the richest aspects of the nightingale's cultural life is its meaningful place in Persian Sufi poetry. Here the nightingale is also very much a bird of love, yet entirely reframed: it is deeply in love with the rose, suggestive of both earthly and spiritual love. Rose and nightingale are depicted together throughout Persian art and verse, and in poetry the association is reinforced by rhyme: *bulbul* (nightingale) and *gul* (rose).[19] In verse, the rose is beautiful, proud and, as its thorns suggest, often cruel, while the nightingale sings its song – sometimes melancholy, sometimes fiery – of longing and devotion for the flower. Again, the nightingale is often a symbol of the poet, and apart from emphasizing the springtime coincidence of rose and nightingale, the symbolism of the bird and flower pulls depictions of the bird well away from the realm of natural history, as intoxicating to the poet as the rose is to the bird itself.

In Farid Ud-Dun Attar's allegorical Sufi poem *The Conference of Birds* (1177), the nightingale represents the all-consuming distraction of earthly love. Each bird in the poem is representative of a human type, and that type's obstacles to enlightenment; for the nightingale, this obstacle is its passion for the rose – it has no interest in spiritual quests:

I am so drowned in love that I can find
No thought of my existence in my mind.
My love is here; the journey you propose
Cannot beguile me from my life – the rose.[20]

Nothing else exists in the nightingale's mind, not even itself, yet it is a melancholy song the bird sings for the rose in an all-encompassing madness. In other Sufi poems, the nightingale is intoxicated by the wine of the rose (wine – *mol* – presents another fitting rhyme), as in 'Red Rose', by Hafiz: dramatizing the rich, intoxicating effect of the subject-matter on the Sufi poet, he writes, 'The nightingales are drunk, wine-red roses appear, / And, Sufis, all around us, happiness is here.'[21]

Back in Britain, in the early modern period, the Philomela myth flooded back into nightingale poetry, with Ovid as the guiding influence. Yet depictions are influenced by Persian myth, too, as the melancholy nightingale came to be depicted singing

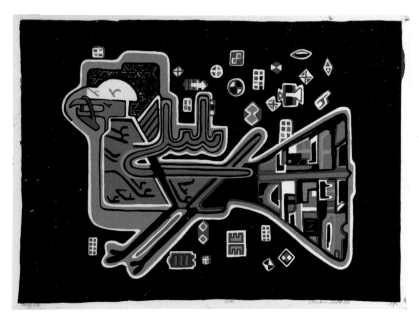

Parviz Tanavoli,
Nightingale
screenprint, 1974.
Tanavoli is known
as the 'Nightingale
of Iran' and
nightingales
are a mainstay
of his works.

with a thorn against its breast. Philomela is not only used as a synonym for the bird, but colours nearly all depictions of the singing bird, which is usually presented as a melancholy female. Ovid's myth had been translated and reworked by Chrétien de Troyes, Chaucer, John Gower and George Gascoigne and, in the Renaissance, Philomela became a more general, yet explicit symbol of the poet in a setting poised between melancholy spring topoi and natural environment, the song steeped in a unique brand of spring-inspired creative melancholy.

This can be seen in Sir Philip Sidney's 'The Nightingale' (1595):

The nightingale, as soon as April bringeth
Unto her rested sense a perfect waking,
While late bare earth, proud of new clothing, springeth,

Sings out her woes, a thorn her song-book making,
And mournfully bewailing,
Her throat in tunes expresseth
What grief her breast oppresseth
For Tereus' force on her chaste will prevailing.
O Philomela fair, O take some gladness,
That here is juster cause of plaintful sadness:
Thine earth now springs, mine fadeth;
Thy thorn without, my thorn my heart invadeth.[22]

While it is coloured by mournfulness, the poem is full of arrivals and awakenings – the new clothing of the earth, the making of a songbook – and Philomela's pain is almost glorified in the celebrated expression it facilitates, dramatized in the thorn image. In Shakespeare's Ovidian 'The Rape of Lucrece' (1594), Lucrece invokes 'Philomel', who 'against a thorn thou bear'st thy part, / To keep thy sharp woes waking', and it became a proverb at this time 'to sing like a nightingale with a thorn in her breast'.[23] The thorn also came to have some sexual connotations through a pun on its 'prick'.

The provenance of the nightingale–thorn association cannot only be attributed to the connection of the bird with the rose in Persian poetry but possibly to the nightingale's real-life habitat of thorny scrub. In his 1646 *Enquiries into Vulgar and Common Errors*, Sir Thomas Browne wondered whether the poetic image of the woeful nightingale sitting with its breast against a thorn may more accurately be understood by the bird's decision to roost in thorny and prickly places to deter predators. Sometimes it's difficult to tell where natural history ends and mythologization begins.

While the nightingale's poetic history is vast, it is marked by turning points: significant poems and poets that have had particular resonance and influence. After Ovid, the next poetical turning point is John Milton (Coleridge, Keats and T. S. Eliot are at the helm of later generations). While almost every poet of the sixteenth and seventeenth centuries writes of the nightingale, it is Milton who came to be most powerfully associated with the bird. From his earliest writings to his epic *Paradise Lost* (1667), the nightingale features in much of Milton's verse. As Pennant noted in his *British Zoology*, the nightingale was 'the favourite bird of the British poet, who omits no opportunity of introducing it',

Frontispiece of Catulle Mendès, *Philomela, livre lyrique*, etching by Félix Bracquemond (1833–1914).

and quotations from Milton's poetry fill Pennant's chapter on the nightingale. The bird that sings by darkness had special resonance for the blind poet, manifesting in the celebrated, beautiful invocation to light in book III of *Paradise Lost*, in which the poet is likened to the nightingale (as well as other blind prophets and poets), in his nightly visitations to the fountains of 'sacred song':

> Then feed on thoughts, that voluntary move
> Harmonious numbers; as the wakeful Bird
> Sings darkling, and in shadiest Covert hid
> Tunes her nocturnal note.[24]

It is a major and influential declaration of the nightingale as divine muse-poet. Within the narrative of the poem, the nightingale is the bird of Eden, serenading Adam and Eve in shameless nuptial life and lovemaking, and lulling them to sleep.

However, it is Milton's 'Il Penseroso' (1645) that had the strongest influence on the nightingale's cultural life in the decades that followed. In the poem, the bird is 'Philomel', yet Milton mutes the Ovidian tale, and the bird instead brings with it a general mood of melancholy, 'Sweet bird, that shunn'st the noise of folly, / Most musical, most melancholy!'[25] There are no vestiges of violence or grief, no thorn or deep 'old-world pain'. Philomel's realm here is one of moonlight, welcoming woodland and a sweet, gentle sadness. The poem's title means 'the contemplative man', and the speaker is a solitary figure of sensibility, who, like the nightingale, shuns 'folly', and claims the evening as a time of introspection and inspiration, and the secluded woodland as the place for it. The poem coloured much of the verse of Milton's eighteenth-century admirers, suffused with its melancholy, meditative mood. In a 1746 ode, Joseph Warton addresses the nightingale as 'CONTEMPLATION's favourite bird', 'that to the moon-light vale /

Warblest oft thy plaintive tale' and invokes its song to the spirit of the poem, imploring 'sweet PHILOMEL' to 'In sympathetic numbers join / Thy pangs of luckless love with mine!'[26]

Inspired by Milton, with the poet as the speaking 'I', wandering alone in woodland or vale, there is an increasing sense of getting closer to the 'real' nightingale in the eighteenth century, yet invocations of the bird as muse or poet still often serve to distract from it. Nightingales feature in a number of poems by James Thomson, a poet who was widely celebrated for his accurate portrayals of the natural world, including by John Aikin in *An Essay on the Application of Natural History to Poetry* (1777). The chief aim of Aikin's essay is 'to shew that the accurate and scientific study of

Parviz Tanavoli, *Bird and Tree*, 2004, bronze sculpture.

Nightingale in song.

nature would obviate many of the defects usually discoverable in poetical compositions'.[27] Defects such as 'supineness and servile imitation' can be redressed by turning to the natural world, he suggests, with a new attention to and emphasis on precision and accuracy. Aikin complains of the false and erroneous images of nature to which traditional poetic imagery and language have led: 'false representations of natural things, the real properties of which are commonly known . . . cannot stand the test of sound criticism.'[28] Thomson is identified as an exception among poets guilty of false representation and imitation, 'The Naturalist's Poet', according to Aikin, who quotes a popular nightingale passage from Thomson's *Spring* (1728):

> Up-springs the lark,
> Shrill-voiced, and loud, the messenger of morn;
> Ere yet the shadows fly, he mounted sings
> Amid the dawning clouds, and from their haunts
> Calls up the tuneful nations. Every copse
> Deep-tangled, tree irregular, and bush
> Bending with dewy moisture, o'er the heads
> Of the coy quiristers that lodge within,
> Are prodigal of harmony. The thrush
> And wood-lark, o'er the kind-contending throng
> Superior heard, run through the sweetest length
> Of notes; when listening Philomela deigns
> To let them joy, and purposes, in thought
> Elate, to make her night excel their day.
> The black-bird whistles from the thorny brake;
> The mellow bullfinch answers from the grove:
> Nor are the linnets, o'er the flowering furze
> Pour'd out profusely, silent.[29]

These are joined by the jay, rook, daw and stock dove. The nightingale stands out here, however, as the only bird not to be named, appearing instead as 'Philomela' – and it is also the only bird to be characterized as female. At the beginning of this section of *Spring*, Thomson includes a typical invocation of the song of the nightingale to the spirit of the poem:

Lend me your song, ye nightingales! oh, pour
The mazy-running soul of melody
Into my various verse! While I deduce,
From the first note the hollow cuckoo sings,
The symphony of spring.[30]

The way in which Thomson's speaker keenly 'deduces' the first note of the cuckoo contrasts with the interest in the nightingale. Its role is in channelling a vague, poetic 'mazy-running soul of melody', while Thomson pays closer attention to other species. Special rules seem to apply to the nightingale. Indeed, in his essay, Aikin points to a 'slight error' Thomson makes about the bullfinch in deeming its song to be mellow, yet Aikin does not mention the mythological trappings of the nightingale.

In 1798 there came another major turning point in the cultural life of the nightingale, with Samuel Taylor Coleridge's 'The Nightingale: A Conversation Poem'. It was published in *Lyrical Ballads*, the collection of poems by William Wordsworth and Coleridge often considered the landmark publication of the Romantic movement. 'The Nightingale' was the product of spring days spent with William and Dorothy Wordsworth in Somerset, walking on the Quantocks and hearing nightingales sing. Located firmly outdoors, Coleridge's poem seeks to undo the connection between the nightingale and the melancholic, and poetic tradition more widely:

> And hark! the Nightingale begins its song,
> 'Most musical, most melancholy' Bird!
> A melancholy Bird? O idle thought!
> In nature there is nothing melancholy.[31]

Rather than echoing the conceits of tradition, poets would be much better off, he suggests, stretching out 'Beside a brook in mossy forest-dell' and listening to the real bird's song. Coleridge casts aside notions of 'Philomela's pity-pleasing strains' (the stuff of theatres and ballrooms) and promotes 'a different lore':

> 'Tis the merry Nightingale
> That crowds, and hurries, and precipitates
> With fast thick warble his delicious notes,
> As he were fearful that an April night
> Would be too short for him to utter forth
> His love-chant and disburthen his soul
> Of all its music![32]

Thus Coleridge's poem gives us the male, supposed merry, nightingale as a response and a corrective to the poems that preceded it.

Some years after 'The Nightingale' was written, Coleridge and Keats met on Hampstead Heath in April 1819. One of the things they discussed was nightingales and poetry, perhaps hearing the birds sing as they walked.[33] Coleridge wrote of how they were incessant as frogs that spring in the Highgate and Hampstead area, and Keats composed his great ode in response to a bird that was nesting in the Hampstead garden of his lodgings with Charles Brown at Wentworth Place (now Keats House, a museum). In part, Keats's ode responds to Coleridge's call to poets to surrender their whole spirit to the song of the nightingale. For Keats, however, this results in a very different poem from that of his predecessor. Again, though, the bird is happy, a 'light-winged Dryad of the trees', which

Wentworth Place, now known as Keats House, Hampstead. Keats composed his famous ode under the plum tree in the garden.

> In some melodious plot
> Of beechen green, and shadows numberless,
> Singest of summer in full-throated ease.[34]

The poem is set at deep night, shrouded in 'embalmed darkness', in which the nightingale is a 'darkling' (a borrowing from Milton). The poem grows to a crescendo, until:

> Now more than ever seems it rich to die,
> To cease upon the midnight with no pain,
> While thou art pouring forth thy soul abroad
> In such an ecstasy![35]

The ode shifts beautifully between the real bird singing in the natural world (known, and felt, but unseen in the darkness), and its more visible, rich cultural life, between 'the voice I hear this passing night' and the 'self-same song' heard down the ages:

> Thou wast not born for death, immortal Bird!
>   No hungry generations tread thee down;
> The voice I hear this passing night was heard
>   In ancient days by emperor and clown:
> Perhaps the self-same song that found a path
> Through the sad heart of Ruth, when, sick for home,
> She stood in tears amid the alien corn;
> The same that oft-times hath
> Charm'd magic casements, opening on the foam
> Of perilous seas, in faery lands forlorn.[36]

Joseph Severn,
*Keats Listening to
the Nightingale on
Hampstead Heath*,
1849, oil on canvas.

It is this for which the poem is celebrated. As Mabey writes, 'To have caught the tension – and the resonance – between the

immortal nightingale of the imagination and the flesh-and-blood bird is one of the poem's great achievements'.[37]

As the poem recedes, so does the bird's song: now an elegiac 'plaintive anthem', which fades

Past the near meadows, over the still stream,
Up the hill-side; and now 'tis buried deep
In the next valley-glades[.][38]

With the final lines, it becomes impossible to distinguish between Keats's imaginative flight and the nightingale's song, to tell which cheats and fades as the poem ends.

It is generally accepted that Keats 'did something to the nightingale', as Tim Dee – birdwatcher and author who writes beautifully on the nightingale – says, and his ode has had an astonishing influence on subsequent writing and thinking about nightingales.[39] All poems on the bird written in its wake respond in some way to Keats's ode. One contemporary example is 'The Nightingales Nest' by John Clare, the great Northamptonshire labouring-class poet and powerfully distinctive writer of the natural world. In his 'natural history' letters, Clare writes with exasperation of the myths and inaccuracies attached to the nightingale, of those who puzzle over whether nightingales sing by day and night and whether their song is 'grave or gay'. He offers an explanation: 'the poets indulgd in fancys but they did not wish that those matter of fact men the Naturalists should take them for facts upon their credit.'[40] Here Clare signals to the way in which works of natural history have drawn on and included elements of poetry, as seen from Pliny to Pennant and beyond. According to Clare, one should look on nature with a specific 'poetic feeling', to be distinguished from 'fancy', and aspire to an accuracy and field-based authenticity that is removed from the cold, dry treatment of the scientist.[41]

This manifests in 'The Nightingales Nest', one of several poems he wrote on the bird. The reader is taken 'Up this green woodland' to hear the nightingale – and indeed to see it – 'Creeping on hands & knees through matted thorns' to find the nest. The poem is underpinned by an awareness of poetic tradition, but proximity to the bird cuts through it:

> her renown
> Hath made me marvel that so famed a bird
> Should have no better dress than russet brown.[42]

As such, this earthbound, daytime poem gives us the first real visual depiction of the singing bird in poetry, a significant departure from all the night-time sound poems of invisible inspiration. Again, the bird is happy here:

> Her wings would tremble in her ecstasy,
> And feathers stand on end, as 'twere with joy,
> And mouth wide open to release her heart.[43]

Nightingale nest with eggs.

The poem ends with a detailed first-hand description of the nest – 'dead oaken leaves', 'velvet moss', grass, down and hair – to rival any natural history prose. Inside, 'Snug lie her curious eggs in number five, / Of deadened green, or rather olive brown.' Clare's earthbound approach contrasts with that of Keats, whose speaker is unable to see what flowers (of a cultivated garden) are at his feet or the bird itself. Indeed, Clare wrote of Keats,

> his descriptions of senery [sic] are often very fine but as it is the case with other inhabitants of great citys he often described nature as she . . . appeared to his fancys & not as he would have described her if he had witnessed the things he describes.[44]

There is, however, an aspect of Clare's poem that problematizes his own emphasis on accuracy, for in 'The Nightingales Nest', the singing bird is presented as female. This is despite Clare's own 'witnessing' and observation: 'I watched her [the nightingale] frequently,' he writes in a prose note, and 'as regards particulars this is in the wrong gender for I think and am almost certain that the female is silent & never sings.'[45] In his other nightingale poems, Clare sometimes presents the singing nightingale as female, sometimes as male. It seems somewhat fitting that the moment we are taken so close to the 'real' nightingale – guided by Clare's naturalist's knowledge – that it again eludes us. The nightingale's cultural identity, formed by the 'fancy' of poets, is so powerful that it transcends the evidence of first-hand observation. Clare's poem is perhaps just as accurate in knowingly mistaking the gender of the bird, honouring its life of 'fame' as much as details of its nest – different, but equally weighted, nightingale truths.

We might think back to Coleridge's nightingale poem, in which he seeks to disentangle the nightingale from literary tradition and

Nightingale singing, in *A Day with Keats* by May (Clarissa Gillington) Byron, illustrated by William James Neatby (1913).

90

myth, promoting the different 'lore' of the natural world. The poem presents something of an impossible project, when literary tradition is so much part of what the bird is about. Coleridge himself acknowledges this in the verse note he included with his poem when he initially sent it to Wordsworth: 'In stale blank verse a subject stale. I send per post my Nightingale,' a statement that undercuts the way he undoes the poetical trappings of the bird within the poem itself.[46] This is perhaps why Keats's ode has had so much resonance, for it transcends, in its way, the knot of nature and culture it is celebrated for holding in dialogue. Coleridge may attempt to undo all the cultural associations of the nightingale, but he replaces them with a different subjective 'lore'. Clare seeks to bring us down to earth again post-Keats, and correct the city poem (while raising new questions of accuracy). Keats doesn't have an agenda, as such. His poem presents the experience of hearing a nightingale, a subjective response in a highly self-conscious poem that focuses on a bird which flits between the here and now, and the immortal life of culture, echoing back Keats's own concerns with life, death and art as it does so.

3 Literary Nightingales: 'Selfsame Song'

Keats's ode changed nightingale poetry at the beginning of the nineteenth century, and has shaped its tradition ever since. After Keats, the tension in poetry has been less between the nightingale of nature and the meanings attached to it – sorrow, love, joy, although these do resurface – and more between the nightingale of nature and literary tradition itself. Keats heard literary tradition in the song of the 'immortal bird' of his ode, and this has been something that poets have continued to hear and write about as they've encountered the nightingale. As explored in this chapter, for Victorian poets such encounters with the nightingale were steeped in passion, while in the twentieth century, the meanings of the nightingale's song, poetic tradition and the lyric voice became fragmented and fractured. More recent nightingale verse has circled back to either the bird's poetic fulcrum or to its origins: some poets have continued to be driven by Keats, while others have inherited the Philomela myth with a new interest in gender.

In the Victorian period, the resonances of Keats's nightingale can be heard in the way poems are underpinned by the poise of the bird between that heard in the present, 'this passing night', and the longer tradition it carries – 'selfsame song' – usually classical in its emphasis. Christina Rossetti's 'Twilight Calm' (1862) echoes Keats in its opening lines: 'Hark! That's the nightingale, / Telling the selfsame tale / Her song told when this ancient earth

Friedrich Wilhelm Keyl, 'Sweet bird! That sing'st away', illustration to William Drummond, 'To a Nightingale', in *The Poets of the Elizabethan Age* (1862).

was young.'[1] This is present-tense listening: an ear to the 'real' bird, yet the tale the nightingale is telling is one already 'told', self-same. In Matthew Arnold's 'Philomela' (1853), the speaker again hears the bird in the here and now: 'Hark! ah, the nightingale – / The tawny-throated!' Yet the nightingale Arnold encounters is a 'wanderer from a Grecian shore', newly arrived from the realm of myth. The nightingale is able to behold the landscapes of both simultaneously: 'Here, through the moonlight on this English grass, / The unfriendly palace in the Thracian wild,' and as the speaker listens to the song bursting through the leaves of the present, he hears 'Eternal passion! / Eternal pain!'[2]

The main quality identified in the nightingale's song in this period is passion, largely without the sexual connotations of earlier periods. There is the 'Eternal passion!' of Arnold's bird, and in 'Twilight Calm', Rossetti refers to 'the passion of her strain'.[3] In Alfred Tennyson's *In Memoriam* (1850), the nightingale knows all about passion – 'O tell me where the passions meet' – and its song is underpinned by opposing passionate forces: 'And in the midmost heart of grief / Thy passion clasps a secret joy.'[4]

94

The elegiac legacy of the nightingale befits Tennyson's great poem of loss. In a note to a different work, Tennyson records hearing a nightingale in a garden in Yorkshire, 'singing with such a frenzy of passion that it was unconscious of everything else . . . I saw its eye flashing and felt the air bubble in my ear through the vibration.'[5] While reminding us of the erstwhile more northerly reaches of the nightingale, the note also points to what is left out in the poetry: the passion is versified, while the less poetic strangeness – and more first-hand, grounded experience, encountering the bird in its natural habitat – of the flashing eye, the air bubble and the vibration are outside poetry's terrain. The nightingale's passion has a different resonance in Elizabeth Barrett Browning's 'Bianca among the Nightingales' (1862). The poem is steeped in landscape and place, yet is deeply coloured with other meanings, viewed as it is through Bianca's remembered love affair in Italy, where nightingales 'throbbed' with passion:

Nightingale singing, Pulborough Brooks, Sussex.

95

The cypress stood up like a church
That night we felt our love would hold,
And saintly moonlight seemed to search
And wash the whole world clean as gold;
The olives crystallized the vales'
Broad slopes until the hills grew strong:
The fire-flies and the nightingales
Throbbed each to either, flame and song.
The nightingales, the nightingales![6]

Each stanza of the poem ends with the nightingale refrain, or a variation on it, and here the bird's sexual connotations rise again – tentatively yet suggestively – to the fore. By the poem's end the nightingales are haunting Bianca back in gloomy England, where her lover has abandoned her for another, and sing now out of spite.

The best-known literary nightingales of this period are not found in verse, however, but in stories by Hans Christian Andersen and Oscar Wilde, in which the nightingale manifests as the ideal subject through which to think about big questions of art and life. Both stories are framed by a central contrast, and in Andersen's 'The Nightingale' (1843), this is between nature and artifice, or more specifically between organic and mechanic sound. The tale is set in China, a 'long, long time ago', where the emperor has established a lavish palace and gardens.[7] Travellers come from all over the world to admire and write about them, yet in their books, what they praise most is the nightingale that can be heard singing there (the subject of 'long odes' by those who write poetry). The emperor seeks out the famed bird and is moved to tears by the sweetness of its song. The bird is brought into the emperor's palace, to serve at the emperor's pleasure, kept in a golden cage.

Common and thrush nightingales, in Johann Andreas Naumann, *Naturgeschichte der Vögel Mitteleuropas*, chromolithographed plate by Fr. Eugen Köhler after B. Geisler (1897).

Illustration by
Mary J. Newill
for Hans Christian
Andersen, 'The
Nightingale',
trans. H. W.
Dulcken (1896).

The nightingale is a hit with the court: people in the street greet each other with the salutations 'night' and 'gale', while twelve shop-keepers name their offspring 'Nightingale'. One day, however, the emperor is sent a mechanical nightingale in the post; silver and gold and studded with jewels, it bewitches the court. The music master declares the superiority of the mechanical nightingale, deeming it infinitely more dependable and knowable, able to keep perfect time and much more pleasing to look at than its predecessor. The real nightingale flees back to the forest. Artifice, logic and mechanism are all pitted against, and prized over, nature's music. One day, however, the mechanical bird breaks and cannot be fully repaired, struggling through its sole annual performance. Five years later the emperor falls ill: death is imminent. The emperor implores the mechanical nightingale to sing, but it remains silent, at which point the real nightingale begins its song from a branch outside the window. The emperor is revived, death is banished, and the bird of nature – organic, vital and life-giving – triumphs. The tale does not end there, however; it takes a moralistic turn, as the nightingale implies that its song will not only help to keep the emperor alive, but will take a role in his rule: 'I shall sing not only of those who are happy but also of those who suffer. I shall sing of the good and of the evil that happen around you, and yet are hidden from you.'[8]

The bird now chooses to be in service to the emperor, and his intention is for him to 'fare . . . better'. The meaning of the moral is not clear. Is the nightingale just a prop to the empire? Or has the tale become about the ethical function of whatever the nightingale represents – beauty, nature, organic music, life-giving being – to be more in touch with real people, and the importance of that to empire? Either way, the power and possibilities of its song are potent indeed.

In some ways, the oppositions Oscar Wilde's 'The Nightingale and the Rose' (1888) explores are similar – music and logic, poetry and rationality – yet the resonances are very different. The nightingale of this tale is more heavily symbolic, and sings, lives and ultimately dies for love, redolent of the bird of Persian myth in its obsession. The story is of a student who is promised a dance with the girl he loves, only if he presents her with a red rose; he despairs

DIE·NACHTIGALL
UND·DIE·ROSE ●●●

at the absence of red roses in the garden setting of the tale. The nightingale immediately takes up his cause, delighted to have found the archetypal 'true lover' of which she has sung 'night after night', telling his story to the night sky: 'What I sing of, he suffers.'[9] Intent on finding a red rose, which seems impossible, the nightingale is offered a solution by the barren rose tree: it is possible for the nightingale herself to conjure a red rose out of its music, stained with its own life-blood. The rose tree instructs the bird: 'You must sing to me with your breast against a thorn. All night long you must sing to me, and the thorn must pierce your heart, and your life-blood must flow into my veins.'[10] The nightingale thinks about it, decides love is more important than life, and agrees. The bird attempts to tell the student, yet there is a fundamental miscommunication between them. Listening to the bird, the student muses: 'She is like most arts . . . all style, without any sincerity. She would not sacrifice herself for others. She thinks merely of music, and everybody knows that the arts are selfish.' The bird's notes, as he hears them, 'do not mean anything, or do any practical good'.[11] The student sleeps as the nightingale sings with her breast against the thorn, singing of love as a newly emerged rose grows crimson. While the nightingale lies dead, the thorn in her heart, the student takes the red rose to his beloved, but she casts it aside in favour of another, more wealthy, suitor. The student quickly recovers, however, and concludes, 'What a silly thing Love is . . . It is not half as useful as Logic for it does not prove anything, [and] is quite unpractical, and, as in this age to be practical is everything, I shall go back to Philosophy and Study Metaphysics.'[12]

The story ends with the student pulling out a 'great dusty book' and beginning to read. The story moves in a different direction from Andersen's 'The Nightingale', in which the bird is heeded, and which ends in resolution and mutual understanding, art

'The Nightingale and the Rose', illustration from *Ein Leben in Schonheit, Oskar Wilde Kalender fur das Jahr 1908* (1907).

and music reconciled. Here, the nightingale is a relic of a bygone time, irrelevant in 'this age' of logic, dying for a worthless cause. The bird's song does, of course, have a practical role to play in the story, unrecognized by the student, but recognized by us. Wilde's sympathy, and ours, lies with the artist-bird sacrificed to misapprehension, beauty and love in an age that doesn't understand it, as practicality is turned on its head.

As the nightingale flits into the poetry of the twentieth century, it still carries its classical inheritance. Yet it is heard differently in the modern age, as both literary tradition and the lyric voice become more fragmented. This is shaped by T. S. Eliot's *The Waste Land* (1922), in which nightingales are subject to the degradation of culture that the poem is interested in. In a vignette in the 'Game of Chess' section of the poem, a piece of artwork depicts 'the change of Philomel, by the barbarous king / So rudely forced.'[13] Seen through the lens of Eliot's version of the modern world, 'still she cried, and still the world pursues, / "Jug Jug" to dirty ears'.[14] In this poem of fragments and echoes, Philomela's celebrated 'jug jug' is reduced by dirty listeners to a bawdy scrap of sound. In Eliot's earlier poem 'Sweeney and the Nightingales' (1919–20), nightingales are again the bridge between the present of the poem and of classical myth. Nightingales sing in the present of the poem, as they sang

> within the bloody wood
> When Agamemnon cried aloud,
> And let their liquid siftings fall
> To stain the stiff dishonoured shroud.[15]

Nightingale by night, Pulborough Brooks, Sussex.

At the end of the poem, the nightingales of the classical world (the reference here is to the murder of Agamemnon) have been drawn into the stained and dishonoured modern world of Sweeney and Eliot, as 'liquid siftings' seem not to describe the nightingales' prized song, but its excrement: it is a long way from the Romantic lyrics of Coleridge, Keats and Clare. Whatever the nightingale's 'liquid' song represented previously, here it has quite literally turned to shit.

A different version of how the nightingale might sound to Modernist ears is given by Mina Loy in 'The Song of the Nightingale Is Like the Scent of Syringa' (1958). Like Eliot's poem, realized in a different way, it is a poem of fragmentation and fallenness. Loy's experimental poem plays with sound and word association, looping around the opening phrase 'nightingale singing', which

Nightingale, from the *Song Birds of the World* series for Allen & Ginter Cigarettes (1890).

is fractured and explored across the short lines ('ing' is repeated in each). Some references are to hearing – 'myringa' is the membrane in the ear that vibrates to sound, 'syringa' itself suggests syrinx – and the poem is an exploration of the sound of the phrase 'nightingale singing', of its own sound as a poem, rather than the nightingale singing.[16] It is Eliot's '"jug jug" to dirty ears' realized differently: far removed from the swelling crescendos and harmonious sound visions of Romantic lyrics, the bird's song is heard and rendered anew.

Elsewhere in twentieth-century verse, Keats still looms large as a predecessor. In 'To the Nightingale' (1911), the Argentinian poet Jorge Luis Borges declared that 'Keats heard your song for everyone, forever.'[17] Ted Hughes titled his nightingale poem simply 'Keats' (1963). Hughes wasn't sure he had ever heard a nightingale – 'I've always lived beyond the bird's pale,' he wrote – yet he still managed to conjure the experience of hearing the bird in his poem.[18] The smack of the real in the poem comes from the pressures of literary tradition and the poet's imaginings, rather than from first-hand experience, complicating how and if we can tell the difference between them.

Keats's poem transmutes across forms, too: F. Scott Fitzgerald's *Tender Is the Night* (1934) takes its title from Keats's ode (in turn picked up by Britpop band Blur's 1999 hit 'Tender'), and the novel is suffused with the language and texture of Keats's poem. While nightingales may befit the French Riviera setting of *Tender Is the Night*, Fitzgerald's mention of the bird singing in the yard of the Buchanan house in *The Great Gatsby* (1925), set on Long Island, is an ecological impossibility in the guise of pathetic fallacy. As an Old World bird, the nightingale has made limited appearances in American literature. In Wallace Stevens's 'Autumn Refrain' (1932), the nightingale is not only 'not a bird for me' but one, determinedly, 'I have never – shall never hear.'[19]

Nightingale,
in William Lewin,
*Birds of Great
Britain with their
Eggs* (1793).

Post-Eliot, the fragmentation of tradition has become a theme in some nightingale poems. In Sujata Bhatt's poem 'History Is a Broken Narrative' (2000), her personal migrations of culture and language, moving from India to the u.s. as a child, are figured through the disjointed narrative of the nightingales encountered in Berlin in the form of a real bird, a myth and a Chinese vase engraved with nightingales. Paul Muldoon's 'Nightingales' (1998) gives us further diverse versions of the bird. The poem begins by quoting Alfred Newton's *Dictionary of Birds* (1893–6), before moving on to tell us that

> I fell in love with a host-face
> that showed not the slightest blemish.
> They tell me her make-up was powdered
>   nightingale-shit.[20]

Muldoon here refers to the Japanese cosmetic product Uguisu No Fun, which translates as 'nightingale faeces'. The excrement is produced not by the nightingale but by the Japanese bush warbler, known as the Japanese nightingale due to the beauty of its spring breeding call. The excrement has been collected in specialist 'nightingale' farms in Japan for centuries and was originally used as a stain remover on kimonos and to remove the thick make-up of geisha. It is now used for blemishes and whitening purposes, and the sanitized powder form is increasingly popular in the West: at least one London spa offers the 'Japanese Nightingale Dropping Facial' at an eye-watering price (at least £180 at the Hilton on Park Lane). Another Japanese reference in Muldoon's poem comes in the form of nightingale floors, which were used in the hallways of temples and palaces as a security measure against intruders due to the squeaking noise they made when walked on. Amid these cultural 'nightingales' is the bird itself, the male bird 'pouring out its soul, particularly during nesting season'. From the bird singing to attract a mate, to floorboards, all are 'nightingales' in their own way, given equal weight and space in the poem. Deryn Rees-Jones's

Nightingale
paperweight.

'Nightingale' (2019) also speaks to the multiplicity of nightingale meanings. These spill out in a dazzling list of different associations in the poem's opening lines, from the adjectival 'brown bird', 'wise bird' and ornithological labels – 'passerine' – to the more abstract phrases of 'box lung' and 'trust hope', and the sounds of 'jazz riff, cello start, / sad techno'.[21] The poem is particularly interested in fragments and parts, as the lines and phrases themselves break and splinter: underscored not so much by the qualities of the nightingale's song, but by what has come to characterize it in all its multifarious meanings and associations.

While tradition may be what many nightingale poems are about, other poems have turned away from cultural nightingales, firmly putting their gaze – or ear – to the nightingale in its natural habitat, or so it seems. A poem by W. S. Merwin, 'Night Singing'

(1996), peels away the layers of literary history – Ovid, Hafiz, Keats – and finds the speaker listening to the nightingale among oak trees in the nothing of darkness, where the only option is to 'listen' and 'ride' the

> long note's
> invisible beam that wells up and bursts from its
> unknown star on on on never returning
> never the same never caught.[22]

Despite its avowed non-literariness, the poem does not only listen, of course. The 'long note's / invisible beam' is rendered visible in the lines of the poem that mimic it: long and unpunctuated, 'on on on', 'never the same', perhaps, but certainly 'caught'. In R. F. Langley's 'To a Nightingale' (2010), a fine, closely observed nature poem, there is no mention of what's being left out, no fanfare for the nightingale. The bird's song enters on the aural field at the poem's end, the last in a litany of closely observed and named Sussex fauna and avifauna: moss, moths, chaffinch, chiffchaff, '*Helina, / Phaonia*', 'Mites which / ramble. Caterpillars which / curl up as question marks':[23]

> Then one note, five times, louder each
> time, followed, after a fraught
> pause, by a soft cuckle of
> wet pebbles, which I could call
> a glottal rattle.[24]

Unlike that which precedes it, the nightingale is not named in the poem. Langley seems careful to avoid any references to its cultural baggage (which might begin with the name). Yet, at the same time, the sound impression becomes increasingly self-conscious and literary. Form and subject blur, as the sounds are suggested through the poem as they are described: the 'fraught / pause' echoes through the line ending and in internal grammatical pauses, while the unusual 'soft cuckle' and 'glottal rattle' ring with onomatopoeic resonance. It would seem that a nightingale poem can't help but be about sound, about making a poem – about itself.

In a mode quite dissimilar to the male naturalist poet, the later decades of the twentieth century also saw a return of the Philomela myth, reworked mainly by women writers in a feminist reclamation of the bird's 'female' voice. It is with these writings that I end the nightingale's literary history, with the present age rounding back upon the cultural bird's origins in the Philomela myth. Some centuries earlier, a number of eighteenth-century women had drawn on the nightingale as poetic subject or persona: Elizabeth Singer Rowe published under the nom de plume 'Philomela', while

Charles Tunnicliffe, *Nightingale*, 1947, watercolour.

Anne Finch, Sarah Nixon, Charlotte Smith, Mary Robinson and Catherine Talbot addressed the bird in their poems. The nightingale has been a complex symbol for the women writers to inherit, steeped as the Philomela myth is in sexual violence against, and silencing of, women. Yet the misconception of the singing bird's sex as female means the bird has been a suggestive symbol of authorship for female poets, poised between being silenced and finding expression. In Anne Finch's poem 'Nocturnal Rêverie' (1713), the night is a special place of meditation and creativity where 'lonely Philomel, still waking, sings', while her

Joseph Wolf
illustration to
Henry Alford,
'A Truant Hour.
Bonn, July 8, 1847',
in *English Sacred
Poetry* (1862).

'To the Nightingale' (1713) begins with a typical invocation of the bird's song to the 'numbers' of the poem:[25]

> Exert thy voice, sweet Harbinger of Spring!
> This Moment is thy Time to Sing,
> This Moment I attend to Praise,
> And set my Numbers to thy Lays.[26]

The poem works upon a competition between poet and nightingale, following the mode of an earlier nightingale poem by Famiamus Strada in which a lutenist competes with a nightingale until the bird loses and expires.

These quietly daring explorations become emboldened in new versions of feminist nightingale lore in the hands of twentieth- and twenty-first-century women writers who reclaim the voice of Philomela. Two such works were for the stage, literally dramatizing the Philomela themes of speaking and silencing: Timberlake Wertenbaker's *The Love of the Nightingale* (1988), commissioned by the Royal Shakespeare Company, and Joanna Laurens's *The Three Birds* (2000), based on a lost play of Sophocles (as per its Greek source, Philomela is a swallow and Procne a nightingale). In her feminist reworking, Wertenbaker develops the character of 'Philomele' into an intelligent, outspoken, sexual young woman, poetic in speech. Wertenbaker has said that the theme of the play is silencing, and how a lack of language leads to violence and brutality.

Margaret Atwood's short story 'Nightingale' (2006) gives the whole telling of the story over to Philomela. It is an abstruse, elliptical re-telling of the Ovid myth, in which Philomela is both nightingale and mythical figure, aware her existence belongs to the realm of story, while having experienced its contents: 'This is when I remember the two of us running, running away from him,

and I know in the dream that I'm dead too, because at the end of the story he killed us both.'[27] At the end of the story, she begins to sing: 'A long liquid song, a high requiem, the story of the story of the story'.[28] Atwood echoes Milton and Keats: the cultural recycling of the bird's song and story are steeped in male literary tradition, and the speaker lives Ovid's tale, yet here, clearly, the song and story is, at last, a female one.

Paisley Rekdal's poetry collection *Nightingale* (2019) addresses more directly the problematic literary inheritance of sexual violence the bird carries. While the poem 'Philomela' contains only a shadow of the original myth, the following 'Nightingale: A Gloss' reflects on the preceding poem, interweaving observations on Ovid, silencing, voice, the nightingale's literary history, its natural history and Rekdal's own experience of sexual violence. The piece speaks powerfully to the nightingale's oldest meanings and how they resonate for the woman poet – and especially the woman poet who has experienced sexual violence – reminding us of the deeply troubling nature of the emblem at the heart of poetry. As Rekdal muses, 'I have spent my life devoted to an art whose foundational symbol is one of unspeakable violence. Did I seek poetry out for this? Or was I, that day in the woods, made into a poet?'[29]

114

The disturbing, deeply held meanings of poetry's 'foundational symbol' and what it means for the woman poet who inherits it are all too relevant in the age of #MeToo. The nightingale's song yields new meanings, then, in both how the song is heard anew, and in how nightingale tradition is experienced and negotiated. This is something to which I return in the final pages of this book, for there is an alternative new relevance of the Philomela myth, with its 'unspeakable violence' and the topoi of loss it has bequeathed to poetry, quite outside of its gendered symbolism: the decline of the real nightingale's song in the UK. It is deep-sunken pain indeed, all ours to sing about, and of our own making.

Embroidery of a singing nightingale.

4 Musical Nightingales: 'Organ of Delight'

Cultural history has insisted that it is poetry that best encapsulates the nightingale, rather than music, despite the clear – albeit complex – affinity birdsong has with the latter to the human ear. This conceit notwithstanding, a huge number of composers have variously evoked the nightingale in their works while musicologists have sought to unlock its secrets, and musicians have insisted on playing to – and with – the bird. Their responses are the subject of this chapter. Birdsong is often deemed to *be* music, yet it cannot, in general, be captured in musical notation, which it transcends in rhythm, pitch, tone and phrasing.[1] While it may be celebrated as the most talented of nature's musicians, the nightingale brings particular challenges to the composer and musician who seek to recreate its song. Some nightingale notes are only a fraction of a second long, and beyond the pitch that the human ear can pick up, while many of the bird's phrases are impossibly rapid: musical imitations of it can be stylistic approximations only. The special relationship between poetry and the nightingale's song is perhaps facilitated by how poetry transcends the complexities surrounding the mimetic possibility – or rather impossibility – music offers. While nightingale poetry is elegiac in subject, nightingale music might be said to be elegiac in *form*: to seek to capture the song in scores, transcriptions and performances is to touch upon it, but to lose it in the

Nightingale, from A. Landsborough Thomson, *Britains Birds and Their Nests* (1910), illustration by George James Rankin.

limitations of human-made music that the nightingale's song will never fail to transcend.

In an old fable, the cuckoo and the nightingale quarrel over who is the better singer. They ask the ass to judge between them (he is deemed to be the best adjudicator thanks to to his long ears). The cuckoo wins: while the ass finds the nightingale's song to be very fine, he finds it dizzying and difficult to understand, preferring instead the more methodical song of the cuckoo. Fellow harbingers of spring, and traditional rivals, the nightingale often appears alongside the cuckoo in musical as well as in literary works, and the birds coincide in two of the earliest examples of the nightingale in music: Johannes Vaillant's fourteenth-century virelai 'Par maintes foys', and Jacob de Senleches' contemporaneous 'En ce gracieux tamps joli'. The vocal line of both pieces mimics the cuckoo and nightingale, which are pitted against each other, and sympathy is established with the nightingale both musically and lyrically. However, a complication arises from the vocal proximity of the two birds – both here and more widely – which could in fact not be more dissimilar. The simple call of the cuckoo is almost the inverse of the complex phrasing of the nightingale's song, yet unlike the nightingale, the cuckoo can be accurately represented in musical form: its call is rare in its correspondence with the intervals of the musical scale, throwing into relief the musically impossible rapidity of the nightingale's notes, and complicating sympathy with it. In Thomas Weelkes's madrigal 'The Nightingale' (1608), the titular bird appears among the blackbird, thrush, lark and cuckoo. Although the nightingale is celebrated as the 'organ of delight' in the madrigal, and gives it its name, the cuckoo accidentally wins in the piece by the way in which it so clearly lends itself to mimesis, both lyrically and musically, sung in its regular interval in the onomatopoeic 'cucu' call that silences the other birds as it rounds off the piece. Only an ass

Noach van der Meer, *Nightingale and the Cuckoo*, 1777, etching.

118

Glottismi modulationum sibilo exprimendi in Luscinia obseruati

Iconismus III.
fol. 30

Pigolismus

Glazismus   Teretismus   Pigolismus

Teretismus   Glazismus

Pigolismus   Glazismus   Chromatico-enharmonicum nescio

quid affectans   Pigolismus   Glazismus

Pigolismus   Pigolismus   Glazismus   Teretismus

Diuersarum uolucrium voces
notis musicis expressæ

Vox parturientis Gallinæ

to to to to to to toto ※ to to to to to to to toto ※

Galliciniũ

Cuchia Cuculicu Cuculicu
Cuchia   A   B

Gallina conuocans pullos
glo glo glo
C

Vox Cuculi

Gucu gucu gucu ※ gucu
E

Vox Coturnicis

Bikebik bikebik bikebik
D

would prefer the cuckoo's song, but this bird is pleasingly hearable, where the nightingale is all dizzy, ungraspable virtuosity.

A more 'scientific' attempt to transcribe birdsong was made by German Jesuit polymath Athanasius Kircher in his *Musurgia universalis* (1650), in which Kircher puts the nightingale's song into musical notation, followed by that of the cock, hen, cuckoo, quail and parrot. The nightingale immediately eludes the framework Kircher brings to it, however: he notes that the nightingale surpasses both the capabilities of any musical instrument and the skill of any musician. In the eighteenth century, the transcription of birdsong took an interesting turn in the form of manuals containing pieces of music by which to teach birds to sing. *The Bird Fancyer's Delight* (1717) for flute and flageolet, for example, contained a number of 'lessons' for caged birds, which included the nightingale as well as woodlark, blackbird, canary, starling and others. Tiny high-pitched recorders, known as bird flageolets, were invented around this time for the purposes of training birds. As the most popular caged bird, the nightingale features heavily in such works, which only went out of fashion with the advent of phonographs and radio. While Daines Barrington found it impossible to put the nightingale's song into musical notation in 1773, some centuries later, in the 1950s, Finnish zoologist Olavi Sotavalta did succeed in transcribing the song of the thrush nightingale. On analysing the song patterns of the bird, he found them to be consistent enough to be formulated into conventional notation, through which he gives a basic structure for the form of nearly all the phrases he found that the bird sang (much less varied than the common species).[2] The emphasis of Sotavalta's scores might be on analysing and quantifying the bird's song, but they have also been taken as scientific evidence that nightingales have a natural aesthetic sense, that they are nature's musicians. Rendering the nightingale's song into musical

Athanasius Kircher, *Musurgia universalis* (1650), musical notation of birds, beginning with the nightingale.

INTRO | ANTECEDENT | BRIDGE (LINK) | CHARACTERISTIC | POSTCEDENT | LINK | FINAL | CADENCE

◄──────────────── PART 1 ────────────────► ◄── PART 2 ──►

Olavi Sotavalta's
structural analysis
of the song of the
thrush nightingale.

notation can both objectively record it and gesture to the bird's capacity for art.

In the 1990s David Hindley transcribed the nightingale's song in a different way, by slowing it down and scoring the new musical landscapes revealed by doing so. Of all the birds he analysed, Hindley found the pitch range of the nightingale's song to be the widest at three-and-a-half octaves (exceeding that of some orchestral musical instruments) and that the fastest distinct nightingale note was $1/149$ of a second, equal to $1/64$ of a note, or a hemidemisemiquaver. In order for the human ear to perceive the song clearly, the song needed to be slowed to quarter speed, and Hindley writes his scores of it at this level. They show the truly dazzling range of the bird's phrases and notes – some of which are sung simultaneously, as enabled by the syrinx and rendered as chords. This strange world of sound can also be heard on Peter Szöke's 1987 LP *The Unknown Music of Birds*. Szöke used a method he called 'sound microscopy', which involved recording birds at half-speed, using a variable-speed tape recorder, and then recording that recording again at half-speed, and so on, with each recording double the length and one octave lower. However, rendering the song more audible to the human ear only serves to transform it into something alien and less like itself. Such attempts to take us closer to the nightingale's song and reveal its fullness, in a sense, only take us further from it (while raising questions about what it is to hear 'truly' the nightingale's song). Yet, as Hindley points out, it is only by slowing down the nightingale's

122

song that its full complexity *can* be perceived. And, in the course of my nightingale research, it is Hindley's work – to which I return at the end of this chapter – that has given me the greatest insight into the experience of hearing the bird in real time, and the power that hearing it has had over us across the centuries.

As well as these more direct transcriptions, other musical works score the nightingale's song in ways that are both literal and more evocative or abstract. One of the best-known musical appearances of the nightingale is in Beethoven's Symphony No. 6, also known as the 'Pastoral Symphony', first performed in 1808. The famous birdsong passage comes at the end of the second movement 'Scene by the Brook'. Beethoven scores the sound of the nightingale (flute), quail (oboe) and cuckoo (clarinet) – species he names on the musical score. The cuckoo is explicitly imitative, while the nightingale's song is necessarily more suggestive, mainly gestured to by the trills of the flute (the less-musical quail is somewhere in between). Beethoven described the symphony as 'a recollection of country life', which he intended to be 'more a matter of feeling than of painting in sounds'.[3] In the birdsong episode, we get a painted glimpse of what a nightingale sounds like (for it can only ever be a glimpse), and a much fuller sense of how it *feels* to hear one as Beethoven scores the differing ways in which a scene by a brook can be 'recollected' through sound.

In the works of the French composer Olivier Messiaen, the nightingale also appears as part of a natural scene transformed into a musical one. Messiaen was a great student of birdsong – working both from discs and birds in the wild – which feature in many of his works. The best known of these is the *Catalogue d'oiseaux* for solo piano, composed in the late 1950s. The nightingale features in book III, 'L'Alouette lulu' (The Woodlark), in a nightscape much darker and more discordant than the gay daytime scene of his predecessor. As Messiaen introduces it,

مرآدهسني برکسنه پهبودولـکه لسانى فضيل اولور • قايني قوزيوب دتى تجزابور
ابكى دونت ادالسنه صايشكدى بيـكرة عداوت واقع اولور فهتره صودنه

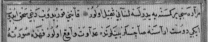

بلبل قادسيـنه هرآد دستان ديرلر • جنه سيـمغيـر • وحركتى سريع • كفى
الالفـاذ وعجيب التغانيـدر • اكتـرنابنا بتبنكـدا آشنالر ابـدر • فجن يرمقدسى
اوئه خلقـدن دنباه بنهان ابـدر • اكم آدمكدكورى طوفـقشه يرمقدس وآنى
تولد ابـدر • زمانه دود ده اغفـاده بيـثلـر • ماداآمكه كلوقنى اوليـه معلوم
اولدز • هرآدبى عاتب زياده اولغله يـراند صغـاربابه ميوب يـيرنـمر صوبنه بگـور
دباغ وقتلكـرده اشنالشون جيـمهبهن فـرياد ابـنزر الحـكم لحـبى سكـره وهرل
خواص لحـبى ده ده جلـده بغلوبپ برکسـنه نلـكـ ساعـده بغلنـه نوع جينـخ ابـدر
• • • مادآمكه اوزڑنه دونومـكطن نهكـره صودنه • • •

يـغمر لسانآن نودركده باايقـونى ديـرلر • كـذو ذا الحطا ابـوبـ آشـنالشون خروج
ابـتـر • شعـث بآمره سى اولده وتبيـون • ودوحـد فى وحرانات مكابـده بيـسود

From the col of the Grand Bois at St-Sauveur en Rue, in the mountains of the Forez. Pinewoods to the right of the road, meadows to the left. High in the sky; in the darkness, the Woodlark peel off two-by-two: a chromatic, fluid descent. Hidden in a thicket, in a clearing in the wood, a Nightingale responds, its biting tremolos set in contrast with the mysterious voice from on high. A Woodlark, invisible, draws near, fades. The trees and fields are dark and still. It is midnight.[4]

Three parts of the scene are represented in the piece: the woodlark, the nightingale and the night. Again, while it is the – here ominous – sense or feeling of the scene that takes precedence, the literal sound of birdsong is nonetheless suggested. Night opens the piece and spreads its darkness, with a sequence of low, slow chords before the woodlark flutters in with the 'fluid' highest notes, while the nightingale's rapid, dissonant 'biting tremolos' (again, it is cast as musician of nature) answer as much to the night as to the woodlark. It is a musical landscape that muddies the distinction between the suggestive and the literal, as we hear the 'sound' of night alongside that of woodlark and nightingale, birds which sometimes 'sound' like their song in the work, but often do not.

Messiaen's approach to birdsong contrasts interestingly with that of Igor Stravinsky, who disagreed with Messiaen that nature was the composer's supreme resource. Stravinsky said that 'imitations' of birdsong such as Messiaen's 'no matter how faithful . . . are necessarily expressed in, cannot escape being contained by, the harmony, rhythm, [and] instrumental colour . . . [of] contemporary musical language'.[5] As in writing about it, making music about birdsong, and in particular the nightingale, provokes enquiry into the relationship between nature and art. The

Ottoman illumination of Zakariya al-Qazwini's *Aja'ib al-makhluqat* (Wonders of Creation), completed in AD 1717 by Muhammad ibn Muhammad Shakir Ruzmah-'i Nathani.

nightingale features in Stravinsky's first opera, *Le Rossignol* (The Nightingale), a musical fairy tale adapted from Hans Christian Andersen's story and first performed in 1914. Adapted to musical form, Andersen's story takes on new meanings. In the opera, the 'real' nightingale is cast as a coloratura soprano, located – with other singers – offstage in the orchestra pit. A small, almost-invisible bird at times appears on stage among the artists and dancers. The mechanical nightingale is depicted instrumentally in the work, creating a contrast between the 'natural' music of the voice and the more objective, crisp and ordered 'mechanic' instrumentation (oboe, piccolo and celesta).[6] In the same interview quoted above, Stravinsky was asked if he thought of 'art' and 'nature' as two realities, and about the transformation of one into the other. His reply is 'For me, music is reality, as I have said before, and like Baudelaire, but unlike Messiaen, "J'aime mieux une boîte à musique qu'un rossignol"' – I prefer the music box to the nightingale.[7] Applied to Stravinsky's opera, Andersen's tale is thus turned on its head, as the mechanical nightingale is recast as the hero of the story, and, in Stravinsky's terms, depicting Andersen's 'real' nightingale in music is an impossibility. While Messiaen's nightingale is nature rendered into art, however that might be done, for Stravinsky there is no nature transformed into music, the only reality is music itself: music box, mechanical nightingale.

A different approach to the nightingale is taken by the Italian composer Ottorino Respighi in his *Pini di Roma* (Pines of Rome), evading the tangle of musicological issues raised by representing birdsong. His symphonic poem for orchestra, completed in 1924, seeks, like Beethoven and Messiaen, to recreate a natural land-scape – or, more specifically, the scenes of four pine trees in the city at different times of the day. Yet, rather than scoring the bird's song, Respighi's score requests a phonograph-recorded nightingale be played at the end of the third movement, 'I pini del Gianicolo, lento' (The Pines of the Janiculum), a nocturne set on Janiculum Hill under a full moon.

The nightingale, along with the song thrush, had been the subject of the first-ever phonograph recording of birds singing in the wild, made by Cherry Kearton in 1900 on an Edison cylinder machine. The nightingale is also the first singing bird to make it onto a gramophone record (10-inch, 78 rpm) in 1910: a recording made by Karl Reich in Berlin from a captive bird. As a result of

Emily Summers, 'Fattengates Chorus', named after one of the best locations on Pulborough Brooks to hear the nightingales: Fattengates Courtyard.

its fame, the nightingale has always been at the vanguard of the latest technological developments: a bird of firsts in attempts to record, and to record birdsong. I like to think of Clare's endeavour to 'take down' the nightingale's notes as an early version of sound recording too. As it opens:

Chee chew chee chew chee
chew chew chew chew chee
– up cheer up cheer up
tweet tweet tweet jug jug jug.[8]

While it has often been observed that no human-made instrument can match the sound of the nightingale, there is an imitative toy instrument called a nightingale, the lower part of which is held in water, which was used in the eighteenth century in an oratorio by Scarlatti, in the 'Toy Symphony' of either Leopold Mozart or Joseph Haydn (authorship is unknown), and, more recently, in Gordon Crosse's *Play Ground* (1977). References abound to recreating the bird's song – often described as 'bubbling' or 'liquid' – using water. Pliny noted the mimicry of the nightingale's song afforded by putting water into slanting reeds and breathing into holes or working the tongue, and in his natural history work *Sylva sylvarum* (1627), Francis Bacon wrote about nightingale pipe, regal or organ, which contained water and made a continuous trembling sound. Throughout musical history, though, it is the human voice and woodwind instruments, especially the flute, that have most often been recruited to represent the nightingale's song – both, like the bird, harnessing breath.[9] The oft-expressed praise or desire to sing or play like a nightingale is curious, however: that wild, hectic, infinitely various yell is often at odds with what

Nightingale whistle.

the nightingale is thought to be – sweet, melodious – when it is heralded in these terms.

Other classical works to feature the nightingale are too numerous to discuss in any detail. There is – by no means an exhaustive list – Johann Pachelbel's playful 'Nachtigall' fugue; oratorios by George Frideric Handel (the ending of the first act of *Solomon* is known as the 'Nightingale Chorus') and Joseph Haydn (the nightingale is named in the aria in Part Two of *The Creation*); a violin sonata by Heinrich Ignaz Franz Biber; and François Couperin's 'Le Rossignol en amour' (The Nightingale in Love), for harpsichord, with imitative trills. Many works set existing nightingale poems and story to music, and include those by Frederick Delius, Edvard Grieg, Johannes Brahms, Franz Schubert, Franz Liszt, Pyotr Ilyich Tchaikovsky, Nikolai Rimsky-Korsakov and Camille Saint-Saëns. The Philomela myth is largely absent from musical tradition, an exception being Milton Babbitt's electronic work *Philomel* (1964), written with the poet John Hollander for soprano, which uses recorded soprano and synthesized sound to do interesting things with the myth's themes of silence, metamorphosis and expression.

The bird is just as prevalent in popular music, which loads the nightingale with further meaning both lyrically and musically. The nightingale's most famous appearance is, of course, in the Second World War hit 'A Nightingale Sang in Berkeley Square', written by entertainer, writer and lyricist Eric Maschwitz, with music by American composer Manning Sherwin and first performed by them in the summer of 1939. It takes its title from that of a short story by Michael Arlen, 'When the Nightingale Sang in Berkeley Square', published in 1923 in the collection *These Charming People*, a satirical take on the decadent London 'fast set' that might find a home on the aristocratic Mayfair square. The story opens in a cutting slight to its pseudo-ornithologists:

Berkeley Square,
Mayfair, London.

There is a tale that is told in London about a nightingale, how it did this and that and, finally, for no apparent reason, rested and sang in Berkeley Square. A well-known poet, critic, and commentator heard it, and it is further alleged that he was sober ... some men have formed a Saint James's Square school of thought, but it was in Berkeley

Square that the poet, critic, and commentator, who was sober, distinctly heard the song of the nightingale.[10]

The nightingale is wholly incidental to the bizarre story of a love triangle that follows, the 'tale' a backdrop to the silly intellectualism of its fast-set world. Turned for less cynical – and infinitely more romantic – ends, Maschwitz's 'A Nightingale Sang in Berkeley Square' officially premiered in the revue *New Faces* at the Comedy Theatre in London, performed by Judy Campbell, in 1940, the same year in which it was first recorded by 'Forces' Sweetheart' Vera Lynn. It soon became a jazz standard and has been recorded by Glenn Miller, Frank Sinatra, Nat King Cole and Blossom Dearie, among many others. The original piece is scored just for piano and voice, but recorded versions spin the romanticism of the song's subject out into swooning orchestration. Strings tend to create the romantic backdrop, while the nightingale is evoked in woodwind detail. Chirping and rapid, running notes of the flute open the Lynn version, becoming more pronounced and more nightingale-like in the trills and flurries of Sinatra's take. The musical suggestion of the nightingale in the piece subtly enhances the meaning of the song's lyrics:

> That certain night, the night we met
> There was magic abroad in the air
> There were angels dining at the Ritz
> And a nightingale sang in Berkeley Square.[11]

The only 'real' aspects of the scene are the meeting, the night, the kiss and Berkeley Square, and the song is otherwise embellished with impossibilities that speak to the proverbial magic of romance.

The song is particularly insistent on the veracity of the nightingale (over dining angels and streets paved with stars):

And, as we kissed and said goodnight,
A nightingale sang in Berkeley Square
I know 'cause I was there
That night in Berkeley Square.

The twittering flute that rounds off the verse in a number of versions gestures towards confirming the presence of the nightingale; the bird is summoned musically in a way that angels and stars can't be: a nightingale sings in 'Berkeley Square' – place and song – as the music actualizes the magical realm evoked lyrically.

The nightingale appears in a number of other jazz standards from the 1940s and '50s as a topos of love and romance. There might be something in jazz as a genre, its unexpectedness and variousness, befitting the nightingale (and it is improvisational jazz that most often gets compared to the nightingale's style). While it doesn't particularly recall the nightingale's song, Oscar Peterson Trio's wordless 'Nightingale' (*Tristeza on Piano*, 1970) conjures the spirit of the bird in the virtuosity shared by pianist and bird. Other works speak to the romance of the bird. 'Midnight Sun' – popular versions include those by Bobby Troup and Ella Fitzgerald – depicts another deeply romantic encounter, in which a lover wonders if they hear the music of the universe or the nightingale. As in 'A Nightingale Sang in Berkeley Square', all seems impossible, yet the nightingale makes the impossibility of romance tangible in its ability to flit between the real and unreal plane: the aural equivalent of stardust on the sleeve, which we, the listener, can hear in the track. Other jazz standards that feature the nightingale include 'If I Knew', written and first recorded by Meredith Williams, but popularized by Nat King Cole in 1962, and 'It Might as Well Be Spring', a Rodgers and Hammerstein number which premiered in their 1945 musical *State Fair*.

Cédric Le Borgne,
Was that a Dream?,
light installation,
Festival LUMIERE,
Berkeley Square,
London, 2018.

The nightingale sings in other genres, too. Julie London tells us in 1957 that 'The Nightingale Can Sing the Blues'. The song clearly exploits the female-singer-as-nightingale trope within a wider grammar – new bird, blue bird – of bird symbolism. The impressions of the lovelorn male are captured in the tough British beat number 'Little Nightingale' by 1960s Manchester band The Mindbenders, who are best known for 'A Groovy Kind of Love', the title track of their 1966 album. The love's less groovy here, as there's a mismatch between the nightingale's sweet song and the snarling mood of the record, which tells of a love gone awry. In 1969 an earlier iteration of Krautrock band Can, Inner Space, provided the soundtrack to a film by Kobi Jaeger, which included the wonderful song 'I'm Hiding My Nightingale from Dawn', with vocals by Margareta Juvan and a suggestive flute (also released as a single). The nightingale reference is baffling, but may have

134

sexual connotations, considering the film is *Kamasutra – Vollendung der Liebe* (Kama Sutra – Perfection of Love), in which a European couple study the Kama Sutra to gain a deeper erotic and spiritual relationship.

In folk music, the emphasis is more on the bird in the natural world. Peter, Paul and Mary's 'Monday Morning' (1965) tells of a nightingale heard in spring and of a fair maiden who sings just as sweetly. The song is in the tradition of the folk song 'Bold Grenadier', also known as 'One Morning in May' (among other titles), the earliest lyrics of which date back to the late seventeenth century. Here, the narrator meets a young maid and grenadier locked in a romantic rendezvous while listening to the nightingale, a scene filled with sexual innuendo. The grenadier accompanies the bird on his fiddle. He is to go away, yet there is the possible promise of a return to hear the nightingale the following spring. In some versions, the maid asks the (already married) soldier to marry her. The song features in the John Schlesinger film adaptation of *Far From the Madding Crowd* (1967) – sung by Isla Cameron – which suggests a tragic ending to the song's story, as it's heard over shots of Fanny Robin's grave and a frantic Sergeant Troy. By contrast, the couple in the Cornish folk song 'Sweet Nightingale' – also known as 'Down in Those Valleys Below' – do marry, and listening to the nightingale clearly takes on sexual connotations, as the married girl is 'no more afraid' to hear the sweet nightingale.

In the singer-songwriter tradition, it has tended to be female vocalists who have sung of the nightingale (although, interestingly, often in songs written, or co-written, by men), matching the singing bird's traditionally misconceived gender. There is Carole King's 'Nightingale' (*Wrap Around Love*, 1974, lyrics by David Palmer), in which the bird, a she, serenades the lonely life of an unnamed he, when his voice is tired, in what sounds like a male fantasy. Again, the flute in the song may gesture to the bird. Anjani Thomas

sings the elegiac 'The Nightingale' on Leonard Cohen's *Dear
Heather* album (2004), a song about a familiar nightingale theme
of death and loss. Unusually, in Norah Jones's jazz-pop 'Nightingale' (*Come Away with Me*, 2002), the emphasis is on the bird's
flight rather than its song, in a plea for an escape. Flight is also a
theme in The Everly Brothers' comeback 'On the Wings of a
Nightingale' (1984), written by Paul McCartney, although here
the emphasis is on the giddiness of love. The nightingale as bird
of love manifests in Julie Cruise's 'The Nightingale' (with lyrics by

David Lynch, performed at the Roadhouse in the pilot episode of *Twin Peaks* in 1990), and Lynch is unusual in getting the gender right in the song, anthropomorphism aside. The nightingale is perhaps most incongruous as muse in Roxy Music's 'Nightingale' (*Siren*, 1975), in which it is implored to form an unlikely duet with the glam-rock outfit, and indeed, the track rounds off with a quiet twittering of birdsong.

One of the more familiar and popular nightingale songs is that sung by Cinderella, or rather, Ilene Woods, in the eponymous 1950 Walt Disney film. We first see wicked step-sisters Anastasia and Drizella taking music lessons, before the scene shifts to Cinderella singing the same song, 'Sing Sweet Nightingale', as she cleans, far more sweetly: we are invited to understand that she is the night-ingale, of course, the sweetness and purity of her voice reflective of her character, in contrast to her mean-spirited, discordant step-sisters. The track is notable for its pioneering pre-Beatles use of double-tracked vocals creating a four-part harmony with Wood's voice.

Christopher Ricks judges Bob Dylan's 'Not Dark Yet' (1997) to be a rewriting of Keats's 'Ode to a Nightingale'. The track doesn't feature the bird, yet other Dylan songs do, and indeed Dylan, winner of the 2016 Nobel Prize in Literature, might be expected to engage with this most literary of subjects. Some live performances of one of Dylan's most celebrated songs lyrically, 'Visions of Johanna' (1966), have the additional line in the fifth verse, 'He examines the nightingale's code', while in 'Jokerman', from the 1983 *Infidels* album, Dylan sings 'Jokerman dance to the nightingale tune, / Bird fly high by the light of the moon.'[12] Both songs are lyrically elusive and nebulous – qualities in which the nightingale plays its part. 'Jokerman' is probably a song about Dylan himself: a mythic, trickster figure who dances to the song of the nightingale, a fellow unknowable artist, while the secret line of 'Visions of Johanna' is its backstory, hinting at the interest in knowing the bird's secrets. Both references have provided the titles of studies of Dylan's lyrics – Aidan Day's *Jokerman* and John Gibbens's *The Nightingale's Code* – which might say something about their suggestiveness and relevance to Dylan's art.

Unsurprisingly, musical groups have appropriated the name of nature's most prized songbird. The Dixie Nightingales (also known as Ollie & the Nightingales and The Nightingales), based in Memphis, Tennessee, were one of the most successful Southern gospel groups of the 1950s and '60s. Lead singer Ollie Hoskins later went on to pursue a solo career as 'Ollie Nightingale'. The Sensational Nightingales are another gospel group, popular in the 1950s, who continue to tour. A more ironic appropriation seems to be the British post-punk group The Nightingales, which formed in 1979. There is also the Danish Nightingale String Quartet, founded in 2007, and no doubt countless other iterations of musical groups and choirs.

There is another story in the history of nightingale music, and one of the most famous aspects of this bird's cultural life. The story begins one balmy spring night in 1923, when Beatrice Harrison took her cello into the woods behind her home at Foyle in Limpsfield, Surrey, England, and began to play amid the blue-bells and primroses: 'Suddenly a glorious note echoed the notes of the cello. I then trilled up and down the instrument, up to the top and down again: the voice of the bird followed me in thirds! I had never heard such a bird's song before – to me it seemed like a miracle.'[13]

Harrison continued to play with the nightingale – for a night-ingale it was – throughout the spring until it left in June. The following year, the 'heavenly voice' was back, and Harrison was inspired to share the experience beyond her audience of rabbits and shrews. She took her idea to Sir John Reith who, after some

W. Seaby,
'The Nightingale',
in W. Beach
Thomas and
A. K. Collet,
*Birds Through
the Year* (1922).

persuasion, agreed to record her duet with the bird for BBC radio, in the world's first outdoor radio broadcast. Harrison began by playing Edward Elgar, Antonín Dvořák and 'Danny Boy' without any luck, yet at a quarter to eleven on the night of 19 May 1924, the bird piped up to Rimsky-Korsakov's 'Chant hindou'. The broadcast was heard by over a million people around the world, and, as Harrison writes, 'the public . . . went completely mad' over

Beatrice Harrison duetting with nightingales.

the performance: 'the experiment touched a chord in their love of music, nature and loveliness.'[14] She received thousands of letters of appreciation, many addressed to the 'Lady of the Nightingales' or the 'Nightingale Lady'. Soon after, Reith wrote in the *Radio Times* that the nightingale 'has swept the country . . . with a wave of something closely akin to emotionalism, and a glamour of romance has flashed across the prosaic round of many a life'.[15] According to some, however, the nightingale on the

Under the gracious patronage of H.R.H. *the* Princess Victoria

SATURDAY MAY 13 at 4 p.m.

in aid of the Royal Society for the Protection of Wild Birds

A NIGHTINGALE FESTIVAL

Organised by **BEATRICE HARRISON** with the kind assistance of the Gramophone Co. (His Master's Voice)

in the famous grounds of

FOYLE RIDING·OXTED·SURREY

The gardens and woods will be open till dawn on Sunday refreshments at low rates available during the whole time

Admission **1s.** Children half-price

BUSES WILL MEET ALL TRAINS AT OXTED STN.

broadcast is not a bird at all, but the well-known bird impression-ist Maude Gould, a story backed up by her grandson.[16] This mattered not to listeners. The 'madness' for Harrison's duets tapped into something quite different from the poetic drive to hymn the nightingale: a need for poetry itself to be heard in the bird, the magic of it, a 'flash of glamour' in a prosaic life. As with

David Rothenberg duetting with nightingales, 2019.

so many aspects of a bird, to believe something about it seems to make it so: a nightingale sang in Berkeley Square, a nightingale sang in a living room.

Harrison's BBC radio nightingale duet was repeated the following month and then every spring for the next twelve years, after which the live nightingale recordings continued without Harrison and her cello. The tradition came to an abrupt end in 1942, in what has become one of the best-known broadcasts in the history of radio, when the live nightingale recording picked up the sound of Wellington and Lancaster bombers flying overhead, en route to a raid on Mannheim, and the recording stopped due to security fears. It's an astonishing moment, the sound of war so starkly opposed to that which touched the public's 'love of music, nature and loveliness'.

Recently, David Rothenberg and Sam Lee have revived the tradition of nightingale duets. Rothenberg has been playing with nightingales since 2014, most recently in Berlin, which has resulted in multiple albums, and, in 2019, a book and film. He thinks of playing with nightingales as 'interspecies music', and, unlike Harrison, responds rather than plays to the bird, mimicking its tones and phrases with bursts and runs of the clarinet, in what sounds like a genuine collaboration. Rothenberg draws on Berlin nightingale research from the 1970s that shows three ways nightingales respond to unfamiliar music, ranging from the aggressive, territorial response, to a more mutual, cooperative scenario that leaves space for the newcomer; this supports his notion of species co-creating 'something no one species could make on its own'.[17] He writes evocatively about the experience of playing with the birds: 'I imagine myself – half man, half bird – strangely poised between nature and technology, darkness and light, dirt and sky. I breathe in and blow out a sound that reaches toward that million-year-old song.'[18]

One of Sam Lee's 'Singing with Nightingales' concerts, Kent, 2017.

In the UK, folk singer Sam Lee has been performing with nightingales for more than five years in Sussex, Kent and Gloucestershire. As 'Singing with Nightingales', he offers exclusive (and expensive) nightingale concerts, which touch a chord of glamour and escapism, much like Harrison's duets. Lee gathers small audiences at secret locations for stories around a campfire, before guests are led into the woods to hear Lee, among other musicians, duet with the nightingale.

In contrast to Rothenberg, always seeking the new in his musical enterprises even as he reaches towards that million-year-old song, Lee frames his project in an ancient folk tradition. In singing with nightingales and reviving folk songs of the past, he seeks to restore the more 'coexistent' relationship with nature and the land that is written into those songs, a process he mysteriously calls 'the "broadcasting" of sonic heirloom seeds'.[19]

These duets tell us little about the bird, its song or what has driven the obsession with it. The nightingale re-caged? While the context has clearly shifted, not least outside (audiences go out to the bird's habitat rather than bringing it into their own homes), and into a new language of 'interspecies' and 'coexistence', these collaborations still bring the bird into our service, enlisting it for our art and delight. In England, it seems a particularly peculiar type of entertainment – the worth and magic of the experience notwithstanding – to go to the nesting territories of a bird on its way to extinction in the UK, its song ever a 'small hymn to survival', to play it music.[20] The birds, of course, go on regardless, and the ways in which music, and other art forms, come to the service of the bird – an enterprise that Lee is at the heart of – is discussed in my final chapter.

To me, it is Hindley's musical experiments that yield the greatest insights into the nightingale's song. In the introduction to this book, I wrote about the feeling of senses working differently

when hearing the nightingale, of something beyond what the ear can hear, something beyond its grasp. In slowing down the nightingale's song, Hindley evidences this by showing that much of it is beyond the human range of aural perception: the range and speed of many nightingale phrases 'merge into undefined twitter' to the human ear.[21] He contrasts this with the song of other popular birds such as the song thrush, blackbird and blackcap, which 'fit more comfortably into our range of aural perception'.[22] What we hear when listening to the nightingale's song is only partial, cursory and perfunctory, a teasing suggestion of the musical spoils compressed within. This is perhaps at the root of our obsession with the nightingale: its lure lies in its essential inaudibility, an unwitting frustration of hearing and sense of something beyond. Is it this that has driven the relentless chase of words and music?

E. F.

5 'Immortal Bird'? Nightingales in Decline

As well as shaping the nightingale's meanings as a bird, humans have determined its ecological life, and this is no more apparent than in the current age of the Anthropocene, of global heating and mass biodiversity loss – Earth's current and future life written by human activity. The shrinking of Britain's nightingale population to fewer than 5,500 pairs (a decrease of 93 per cent over the past fifty years) is one of the biggest declines of bird breeding in the UK since records began. If current trends continue, the nightingale could become extinct as a British breeding bird by the year 2025. In 1963 Aldous Huxley asked, 'In this second half of the twentieth century what should a literary artist, writing in the English language, do about nightingales?'[1] As nightingales decline, so does 'the biological basis', he writes, 'for a long tradition of poetical feeling and poetical expression'.[2] Indeed, what might nightingale loss mean for literary tradition? And what might cultural history mean and do for the nightingale, as it heads towards extinction in a country that has been so enthralled by it, and which has, in a sense, made it into what it is? This, my final chapter, explores the nightingale's decline in the UK, as well as hopes for its future, and ends by reconsidering the bird's literary life, nature–culture relations rendered anew, in this current age of loss and hope.

The nightingale has been on the UK Birds of Conservation Concern 4: Red List since 2015 (although it warranted a place on

Nightingale from W. Swaysland, *Familiar Wild Birds* (1883), illustrations by Archibald Thorburn and Eliza Turck.

it earlier) – the highest conservation priority, with species listed requiring urgent action. Both the common and thrush nightingale are on the European Red List, yet are in the category of least concern, remaining – in recent years – relatively stable, especially in central Europe.[3] For the whole of Europe, the long-term trend (1980–2016) is of moderate decline, yet the short-term trend (2007–16) is of a moderate increase.[4]

The most pressing issue for nightingales in the UK is loss of habitat. There is almost no natural scrubland – the bird's preferred habitat – left in our landscapes, obsessed as the British are with tidiness, neatness and rolling green fields. The story of the nightingale's habitat in the UK has been determined by human activity and demand for goods, and is bound up with the fortunes of both scrub and the ancient woodland management practice of coppicing. In her book *Wilding* – discussed further below – Isabella Tree writes powerfully on the fate of scrub in the UK, rendered 'supposedly useless' and 'demonized' in the twentieth century:

Nightingale on a sign at RSPB Pulborough Brooks reserve, a 'hotspot' for the birds in the UK.

Once, untidy margins were tolerated, even encouraged.
Now, armed with motorized tools, we have become a nation
obsessed with orderliness and boundaries . . . A patchwork
of neatly hedged fields dotted with mature trees and small
copses, framed by bare, rolling hills and slow-flowing rivers
has become the archetype of England's green and pleasant
land. It is etched in our subconscious, the bar-code of stab-
ility, prosperity, control. Rooted in this idyll is our notion
of mankind, subjugator of wilderness, bending nature to
our sway.[5]

One British obsession is incompatible with another: the poetic
love for the nightingale and this sense of how the English 'landscape' should look. In addition to aesthetics, productivity and
usefulness play their part. Scrub was also once very highly valued,
with – from at least the medieval period – species such as blackthorn, hazel, hawthorn, alder, dogwood and gorse put to many

uses: from tools, firewood and gunpowder to food, medicines and dyes. Yet, in the present day, scrub is undervalued by both the public and conservationists, perceived as an unproductive wasteland, as well as unpleasing to the eye.

The practice of coppicing has also been driven by demand – for woodland products of firewood, fencing and construction timber. Coppicing involves felling trees near to the ground, engendering the re-growth of the young, dense shoots for future cropping, providing a scrub-like habitat – Mabey calls coppiced woodland 'scrub's simulacrum'. While scrub is the nightingale's original habitat, coppiced woodland, which creates similarly dense vegetation close to the ground, has come to be the dominant nesting area of the bird. In recent years, however, woodland has declined in suitability as a breeding site for the nightingale, with the balance shifting back in favour of areas of scrub, the ratio shifting from 25:75 to 50:50.[6] This is partly due to a decrease in coppicing. As Tree records, over the second half of the twentieth century 90 per cent of traditional coppice in the UK disappeared, as ancient coppices – with the demand for woodland products satisfied by cheap plastic alternatives – were left to grow into areas of mature trees or cleared to make way for subsidized farming or development.[7] This has coincided with the decline not only of nightingales, but of populations of marsh tits and garden and willow warblers, as well as butterfly species and hosts of woodland and hedgerow flowers and plants.

An increase in browsing deer populations – Roe, Reeves's Muntjac and Fallow – in lowland England has also depleted remaining coppiced and scrub areas, although this is, in part, due to a lack of other natural areas in which deer might browse and is not uncomplicated, as some browsing can be helpful to maintain the suitability of sites for nightingales. However, studies make clear that deer do have detrimental effects on nightingale populations (and other species), especially in remaining coppiced woodland, and propositions for how to control them are increasingly being put forward, from the reintroduction of lynx or wolves to marketing them as a sustainable source of red meat.[8]

In a book on rewilding Britain and its birds, *Rebirding* (2019), conservationist Benedict Macdonald also brings attention to 'the isolation effect' adversely impacting nightingales, and the phenomenon of 'stochastic extinction' – when a landscape and its birds become so fragmented that normal fluctuations acting on a population conspire to wipe it out:

> The smaller that number of species on an island, the greater the chance that a fluctuation, or 'bad luck' event, will reduce that population to zero . . . Birds like nightingales are designed to take huge losses, but only large populations survive those losses. Once you are left with a tiny population, everything has to work perfectly in order for the species to survive . . . ideal populations of British birds in one place, therefore, should not constitute ten or twenty but at least the low hundreds of pairs.[9]

As Macdonald points out, the nightingale's decline is steeped in the loss of dynamic landscapes in the UK. Britain's birdlife evolved in mosaic habitats, shifting across a landscape over time, especially important for the nightingale whose shrub and woodland habitat is constantly changing and only suitable temporarily. Research shows that nightingales are particularly sensitive to changes in woodland structures. Nightingale populations need to be able to move locally across a large area of scrubland over the course of the passing years, as the landscape continues to evolve. Thus, Macdonald writes, 'It is the piecemeal loss of ecosystem scraps that will ensure the continuing extinction of British birds for decades to come, if conservation does not change. Birds will continue to vanish until we slowly join the scraps back up – into the rich tapestry that nature understands.'[10]

The rare locations in the UK where the nightingale does thrive are not only illuminating on the bird's specific habitat requirements, but lead straight to the heart of vital land-use issues. The most important site for nightingales, and perhaps for the future of biodiversity and environmental policy in the UK, is Knepp, an estate of over 1,400 ha (3,500 ac) in West Sussex. Once intensively farmed, since 2001 Knepp has been devoted to a pioneering rewilding project undertaken by Isabella Tree and her husband, Charles Burrell, the subject of Tree's book *Wilding* (2018). In 1999, a BTO national nightingale survey recorded only nine nightingale territories at Knepp, and by 2001 the bird seemed to have disappeared altogether. However, in 2012, post-rewilding, a survey

Information board detailing nightingale conservation work at Pulborough Brooks RSPB reserve, Sussex.

identified 34 territories: Knepp was now host to nearly 1 per cent of the UK nightingale population. Tree writes:

> Deep inside the exploding skirts of an overgrown hedge, a nightingale's nest . . . identifies why the nightingales are attracted to Knepp. The majority (86%) of the birds had taken up sites in overgrown hedgerows, twenty-five to forty-five feet [7–14 m] deep, where there is around 60 per cent blackthorn with thorny cover extending right to the ground . . . fringed with brambles, nettles and long grasses, and where the cavernous, cathedral-like structure of the thicket's interior offers a safe haven for adults and their fledgling chicks to peck about for insects in the leaf-litter.[11]

The rewilding project at Knepp relinquishes human control and subjugation of the natural world, yielding to 'wilding', and unfurling astonishing results as it does so. Letting nature take its course clearly suits not only the nightingale, but the rare purple emperor butterfly and the turtle dove, among the hundreds of other species that thrum and buzz at Knepp. Importantly, rewilding – by providing that lost dynamic mosaic of habitats again – allows species to move and express themselves, to show where they would rather be, and to thrive there.

Low stock levels of browsing deer and other herbivores help, rather than hinder, nightingale habitat here: areas of scrub (allowed to regenerate before deer were introduced, and thus robust enough to withstand browsing) are prevented from becoming too mature, and browsing cattle in particular foster the tight, scalloped edges that nightingales like. There is no management of vegetation at Knepp, of course, and, unlike traditional conservation, the project is not target-led, or directed at any particular species. It is unclear whether, in the future, the scrub will mature

Charles Collins, watercolour drawing of a pair of common nightingales (from specimens), 1737.

and nightingale habitat will be lost, or if browsing animals will keep it shifting: the outcomes of rewilding are steeped in the unknown, but, so far, nightingale numbers at Knepp are holding, even in years when they have struggled at other sites.

The second important site for the nightingale in the UK is at Lodge Hill on the Hoo Peninsula in Medway, Kent: accidentally rewilded out-of-use Ministry of Defence land made up of woodland and scrub. Between 1870 and 1961, Lodge Hill was an 'ordnance depot' where explosives were stored, and it was subsequently used as a British army training ground. It is now host to rare butterflies, bees and orchids, as well as the largest population of nightingales in the UK. A BTO survey in 2012 found 85 of the nation's 5,500 singing pairs at the site, which was designated as a Site of Special Scientific Interest (SSSI) by Natural England the following year. Julian Hoffman has written about how areas of the base used for bomb-disposal training have become ideal for the nightingale:

> Clear-cuts were mown in parallel lines through scrub where soldiers practised the craft of defusing, leaving unruly thickets to develop between them, unintentionally producing a checkerboard of ideal habitat for nightingales, a suite of dense greenery and clearings, a world of multiple edges where the bird could easily command territory, nest and feed in safety.[12]

Hoffman visits and writes about Lodge Hill in *Irreplaceable*, a celebration of imperilled places and species. 'At a time when writing about the natural world is, of necessity, becoming archival, a record of remembered things that bears witness to continued disappearances', he goes in search of glimmers of flickering resistance, 'light born of a stubborn and unbending refusal to give way

Out-of-use Ministry of Defence land that has been accidentally rewilded, Lodge Hill, Kent.

when the irreplaceable was at stake'.[13] Many of the sites he records are unusual and unique, the fruition of marriage between human intervention and natural processes. It is in these places that nightingales tend to thrive: brownfield sites, flooded gravel pits, former quarries – no man's lands where scrub finds a home. The nightingale's preference for scrubby, unkempt areas is also evidenced by the bird's much-publicized return to the unmanaged city-centre parks of Berlin. Here, unkempt sites, with their dense bushes, piles of leaves and nettles, are home to an estimated number of between 1,300 and 1,700 pairs. It is thought that the nightingale population in the city grew by 6 per cent every year from 2006 to 2016. The birds sing on the sides of roads, heard over traffic at a busy junction, a stone's throw from the Brandenburg Gate. One spring, a bird alighted every night atop a traffic light at the main junction in Alte Treptow. It's a startling contrast to the UK, where the nightingale is experienced as something rare and sublime.

Unlike at Knepp, there are no browsers at Lodge Hill, and the scrub is already on its way to becoming closed canopy woodland, and thus unsuitable for nightingale habitat. Yet there is a greater threat to Lodge Hill nightingales than maturing scrub. In 2011 a planning application was submitted for a development of 5,000 new houses at the site, inspiring one of the largest campaigns in the history of the RSPB. As a result, the number of proposed new houses has since been reduced to five hundred (halting a public enquiry), which would avoid any direct loss of the SSSI, yet serious concerns remain about the levels of houses proposed around the edges of it. Indeed, the nightingale's success at both Knepp and Lodge Hill prompts an appraisal of values. Hostility to the rewilding at Knepp initially arose from an attachment to farming – its ancestry and productivity – and to an idea of how the English landscape should look, as well a concern for rising

populations and for 'wasting' agricultural land. Nightingales were among the birds bemoaned in 2013 by George Osborne as 'feathered obstacles', delaying his plans for economic growth through new infrastructure and building (such as Lodge Hill).[14] The need for starter homes, demand for housing and the debate about where it should be located notwithstanding, the age of devastating biodiversity loss demands that we rethink the capitalist machine of endless striving for growth and productivity, as well as how attached we are to picture-postcard visions of a particular 'green and pleasant' version of English landscape.

Not far from these issues is anthropocentric climate change, to which, on its UK breeding grounds, the nightingale's response has been unexpected. The bird's range – right on its northwestern fringe in the UK – is determined by climate, and had been expected to increase and expand northwards.[15] This has not been the case, however, and the nightingale is one of very few bird species with

Nightingale medallion by Parviz Tanavoli. He sold these works in spring 2020 to help raise funds for hospitals in Iran during the coronavirus pandemic.

157

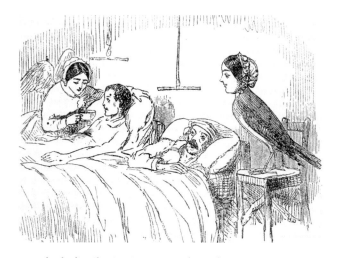

Florence Nightingale in the guise of a bird, from Sarah A. Southall Tooley, *The Life of Florence Nightingale* (1905).

a southerly distribution in Britain to be undergoing a contraction, as well as a reduction, in its prime southeastern range, which seems at odds with global heating. The move northwards of other species has been attributed to climatic warming, and research shows that while there is the potential for the nightingale to increase in abundance within the southern half of Britain, the lack of scrubland habitat means climate change is unlikely to make areas of northern and western Britain suitable for the bird.[16] Climate change could be affecting the nightingale in other ways, as aspects of phenology – the timing of natural phenomena, such as flowerings, fruitions, arrivals, departures – are rendered out of sync. Research shows that some species are nesting earlier in the UK due to warmer springs, while others have not advanced their return migration dates to keep pace with earlier springs, and, on the continent, some species have been shown to have reduced breeding success because they are nesting after the peak availability of caterpillars – themselves synchronized with leaf-breaks on trees – on which they feed. Moreover, a recent study of nightingales in Spain found that climate change has caused nightingales to evolve with shorter wings over the last two decades, a 'maladaptation' meaning shorter-winged birds are less likely to return to their breeding grounds after their first trip to Africa.[17]

Habitat loss and degradation in its wintering sites in Africa are also almost certainly affecting nightingale populations. This is an understudied area, and more research into land use (as well as climate change), and its impact on habitats and bird populations is urgently needed. Intensification and expansion of agriculture; cutting woodland for firewood, charcoal and building materials; and increasing population pressure in western Africa are reducing habitat availability for nightingales, as well as other migrants. There are reports from Ghana of a decline in both fallow farmland matured to form the dense scrub and secondary woodland that the nightingale favours for habitat.[18] Holt et al. also suggest that nightingales may be affected by conditions on the temporary sites the birds use in the arid and semi-arid Sahel or Sudan savannah zones after crossing the Sahara, before continuing to final destinations. A study in Italy found reduced overwinter survival of nightingales following low rainfall in the Sahel, and

WHEN THE Nightingale SINGS...
HELP OUR HEROES
SAVE LIVES.. ♥

'When the nightingale sings': nightingale design in the time of COVID-19 by Madeleine Floyd, 2020.

the steepest decline in British nightingale numbers coincided with crashes in the populations of other Sahelian migrants.[19]

What then for literary history, when this foundational symbol disappears forever from British shores? As Aldous Huxley mused in his book *Literature and Science,*

> The first thing to be remarked is that the spraying of English hedgerows with chemical weed-killers has wiped out most of their population of assorted caterpillars, with the result that caterpillar-eating nightingales . . . have now become rarities in a land where they were once the most widely distributed of poetical raw materials . . . The sprays are used, the weeds are duly destroyed – and so is the biological basis for a long tradition of poetical feeling and poetical expression . . . No weeds, no caterpillars. No caterpillars, no Philomel with melody, no plaintive anthem or charming of magic casements.[20]

Huxley writes at a time when birdwatchers and poets were keenly attuned to declining bird numbers in relation to pesticide use: Rachel Carson's seminal *Silent Spring*, revealing its full horrors over the Atlantic, had been published in 1962. Interestingly, Huxley points to how nightingales are already 'rarities' in 1963, when records – which only begin at this time – put the start of the nightingale's decline to the 1960s. While there isn't the evidence for the direct relationship between chemical weed-killers and nightingale decline Huxley suggests (there are only a few cases where a causative link between insect loss and bird-number declines due to pesticide use has been established), growing relational evidence shows that the decline in insects in the UK – due to pollution, habitat loss and global heating, as well as pesticide use – has caused a catastrophic decline in some bird numbers.[21]

The 'literary problem' of the nightingale Huxley raises (no weeds, no caterpillars, no Philomel, no Keats) gestures to the interrelations between nature and culture, poetry and environment – the remaining focus of this chapter. Other, more recent commentators have brought attention to this too. Mark Cocker writes of how we 'incur systemic cultural loss', along with 'the self-destruction of our land', while Robert Macfarlane asks how artists might respond to and write in the age of the Anthropocene when 'old forms of representation are experiencing drastic new pressures and being tasked with daunting new responsibilities.'[22] While there is a growing swell of environmental elegies in the age of the Anthropocene, I have only come across one nightingale poem specifically about its loss: Peter Reading's untitled poem of 2003. The setting of the poem is the outskirts of Mostar, 'before the bridge was bisected', where nightingales sang, yet no longer do. While the context of the poem may be the Croat–Bosniak War, it feels relevant for present-day English woodlands, and Reading is a powerful poet, writing widely on extinction and environmental loss. Yet, perhaps more powerful to me, an awareness of the age of the sixth mass extinction also brings a new context to 'old', existing poems, songs and 'forms': how might they appear differently and take on new meanings in the current environment of change and loss? For Reading's poem works through Keats's ode, drawing on words and phrases from it: he raises a 'deep-delv'd draught to *Luscinia megarhynchos*', and draws on Keats's elegiac language as the nightingale is experienced through it: 'forlorn, and the very sound seemed / Yes, like a tolling.'[23]

The nightingale's decline also brings Keats to mind for Huxley, yet it needs a revision: the 'immortal bird' has become 'precariously un-immortal, as our recent experience with weed-killers has demonstrated', he notes. Carson's depiction of eerily quiet landscapes in *Silent Spring* is, in a sense, underpinned by Keats's Gothic

Croatian Kuna coin with nightingale design.

Romantic vision in 'La Belle Dame Sans Merci': 'The sedge has wither'd from the lake, / And no birds sing'. The lines are the epigraph for the work, while 'And no Birds sing' gives its title to the central chapter, which tells of how 'spring now comes unheralded by the return of the birds, and the early mornings are strangely silent where once they were filled with the beauty of bird song', although it's the robin that serves as the symbol for the tragic fate of birds.[24] Romantic formulations of the natural world, Gothic and otherwise, give form to environmental values and concerns.

Indeed, in media coverage of the nightingale's decline, its cultural history is nearly always invoked, and it is usually the Romantic lyrics of Coleridge, Keats and Clare – they who heard and articulated the nightingale's song as one of joy. As Patrick Barkham wrote in an article for *The Guardian* in 2016, 'Per-per-per-cheat. Churrup-churrup-chur-put. I'm struggling to put into words the extraordinary song I heard last week. Only poets such as John Keats and John Clare come close to capturing the quick-fire bubbling joy of the nightingale.'[25]

The bird is discussed in relation to the threat to Lodge Hill. To Barkham, the site 'should be a unique national nature reserve': 'Whether it becomes so will say something powerful about our society and whether we always bow to market forces or still have an ear for joy. I'm hopeful. As Keats put it: "Thou wast not born for death, immortal Bird!"'[26]

Such articles themselves say something powerful about the ongoing legacies of Romantic writing, showing how our views of the natural world have been shaped by poets, and the ways in which birds are thus perceived and valued has significant implications for their conservation. It is poetry, alongside – or rather bound up with – the joy of the nightingale that comes down on the side against market forces. Helen Macdonald writes that

'Someone once told me that nightingales should be preserved because of their place in western literature. I suppose that is an argument,' however, she continues, nightingales 'are simply astonishing, in and of themselves'.[27] No one could dispute that, yet it is literature which has enabled us to think and articulate that astonishment, and it can help to preserve it.

While the Romantic nightingale may be recruited for the purposes of joy, in literary history the bird has most often been bound up with loss and mourning, and this tells us much about our relationship with it. The nightingale's founding myths and literary appearances are, of course, elegiac. In the tales of Philomela and Aedon, the nightingale flits between subject and object of mourning, as Ted Hughes's version of Ovid's myth brings out with the help of a line-ending: 'Philomela / Mourned in the forest, a nightingale'.[28] An environmentalist context comes to the fore in Virgil's *Georgics*, which tells of how the nightingale brood is

Tsubaki Chinzan, *Strawberry Spinach and Nightingale*, c. 1845–54.

'pilfered from the nest' by 'some brute ploughboy'. There are also the earlier lines of *Georgics* that speak of 'lands from which a careless farmer carries timber off, laid waste to woods that had stood for years on years and wrecked the ancient habitats of birds'.[29] In the nightingale passage, the bird is explicitly both mourner and mourned as the mother bird sings of her heartbreak, reaching far and wide in an ecology of emotion. These roots of the nightingale's mythologization, in a sense, dramatize our relationship with the natural world. Nightingale poems write the deep connection between humanity and nature, and inscribe closeness, love and kinship, yet that connection is formulated as deep loss.

The nightingale is an innocent victim in countless poems and tales from Virgil onwards. In his twelfth-century work of natural history *De naturis rerum*, Alexander Neckam tells of a nightingale drawn apart by four horses, a burlesque reference, perhaps, to Marie de France's 'Laüstic', in which a nightingale is sacrificed for revenge. The nightingale meets its demise at the hands (talons)

Henry Walker Herrick's illustration of 'The Hawk and the Nightingale', in *The Fables of Aesop: With a Life of the Author* (1869).

of predators in two of Aesop's fables: 'The Hawk and the Nightingale' and 'The Hawk, the Nightingale and the Bird-catcher', in
which the hawk gets its comeuppance. Alcuin of York's ninth-
century poem opens with a lament for his lost nightingale, while
Strada's nightingale duels to the death. Then there is Thomas
Randolph's 'On the Death of a Nightingale' (1638, also the title
– in translation from German – of a musical work by Schubert,
composed in 1816) and William Walsh's 'Upon a Nightingale that
Was Drowned' (or rather takes a suicidal leap into a well, 1721).

Nightingale music is steeped in loss through form, and early nightingale ornithology could also be said to be elegiac, dependent on caged birds that beat themselves to death against their bars as they yielded the secrets of migration. In his *Natural History*, Buffon noted that nightingales 'are delicious food when fat', and the nightingale is still consumed in some areas of the Mediterranean.[30] Oliver Pike reports the different death of a nightingale in his

Illustration of 'The Hawk and the Nightingale' by Aesop, trans. J. Ogilby, etching by W. Hollar (1687).

natural history. He tells of hearing the bird singing from the trenches in the spring of 1916 in a French wood, until a shell bursts beneath it, killing the bird along with five 'brave men'.[31] The nightingale gives an elegiac serenade to the First World War in other accounts. Second Lieutenant Douglas Gillespie describes hearing the bird in Flanders, coming 'all the more sweetly and clearly in the quiet intervals between the bursts of firing':

> There was something infinitely sweet and sad about it, as if the countryside were singing gently back to itself, in the midst of all our noise and confusion and muddy work; so that you felt the nightingale's song was the only real thing which would remain when all the rest was long past and forgotten.[32]

There is an echo of Keats's 'immortal bird' in the way the nightingale transcends human mortality as it laments man's degradations, its poignant juxtaposition of sound pre-echoing that of the Wellington bombers heard over nightingale song on British soil in the 1942 BBC radio broadcast (and, in a different way, the war-time escapism of 'A Nightingale Sang in Berkeley Square'). Gillespie himself was killed in 1915, aged 26, on the first day of the Battle of Loos (for 'youth grows pale, and spectre-thin, and dies'). Others found the song heartening – 'miraculous after the desolation of the trenches', said Siegfried Sassoon – or heard in birdsong an echo of English pastoral and the tug of homesickness in 'English' birds.[33]

James Thomson's 'Spring' (1728) provides an earlier example of the new meanings that existing nightingale poems take on as environmental contexts shift, in lines which rework Virgil's famous *Georgics* passage to speak to eighteenth-century concerns of the caged-bird trade. Poetry should not shy away from such matters:

The Nightingale, in *Bewick's Select Fables of Aesop and Others* (1871).

Be not the Muse ashamed, here to bemoan
Her brothers of the grove by tyrant Man
Inhuman caught, and in the narrow cage
From liberty confined . . .[34]

'Friends of love' are implored to 'spare the soft tribes, this barbarous art forbear!'[35] The poem turns specifically to the nightingale, as Virgil's pilfering 'brute ploughboy' becomes the harder 'unrelenting clowns' who 'rob' from the nest:

But let not chief the nightingale lament
Her ruined care, too delicately framed
To brook the harsh confinement of the cage.
Oft when, returning with her loaded bill,
The astonished mother finds a vacant nest,
By the hard hand of unrelenting clowns
Robbed, to the ground the vain provision falls;

168

Her pinions ruffle, and, low-drooping, scarce
Can bear the mourner to the poplar shade;
Where, all abandoned to despair, she sings
Her sorrows through the night; and, on the bough,
Sole-sitting, still at every dying fall
Takes up again her lamentable strain
Of winding woe . . .[36]

The lines were widely known and quoted throughout the eighteenth century, appearing in a number of essays and works bemoaning the caging of birds, in an emergent animal rights discourse. While this section of Thomson's *Spring* implies a poetic sympathy with the bird, the poet partaking in its 'winding woe', the nightingale, as discussed in Chapter Two, also elsewhere appears as Philomela in the dawn chorus, and is called upon to underpin the poem in a typical invocation to nightingales to 'pour / The mazy-running soul of melody / Into my varied verse!' *Spring* is steeped in the nightingale weave of kinship, elegy, environment and environmental loss in the inspiration it takes from the bird's song, which we might call the weave of poetry itself.

The caged bird trade certainly contributed to local declines of the nightingale in the eighteenth and nineteenth centuries. In *Birds of Middlesex* (1866), James Harting records how the nightingale 'is now by no means so common in the county as formerly' – not surprising when a Middlesex gamekeeper caught 180 nightingales there in one season alone. In the same year, Richard Jefferies wrote of how 'a couple of roughs would come down and silence a whole grove . . . The mortality was pitiable, seventy percent of these little creatures that were singing a week before in full-throated ease in the Surrey lanes would be flung into the gutters of Seven Dials or Whitechapel.'[37] The reference to Keats brings home what is being lost. It wasn't until a succession of wild bird protection acts began in 1880, driven by early iterations of the RSPB, that the trade was slowly disassembled. In 1933 Beatrice Harrison held a 'Nightingale Festival' at Foyle Riding – she performed and Oliver Pike gave a lecture – for the purpose of collecting signatures in support of Lord Buckmaster's proposed amendments to the bird protection legislation centred on caged birds, as well as for raising money for the RSPB. In spring 2019, nightingales and music brought people together in support of nature in a different way, in the form of an Extinction Rebellion event in Berkeley Square. Hosted by Sam Lee, it was advertised as a 'rewilding' of the square with the song it is most famous for, in a celebratory and peaceful finale to the two weeks of climate protests that had blockaded junctions in London. A crowd of 750 people gathered as the nightingale's song was streamed via mobile phones and speakers, partaking in a mass rendition of 'A Nightingale Sang in Berkeley Square', with amended lyrics ('angels forsook the Ritz and took to the streets in protest').

A nightingale rebel at the Extinction Rebellion 'A Nightingale Sang in Berkeley Square' event, 2019.

To the environmentalist and writer Michael McCarthy, 'A Nightingale Sang in Berkeley Square' has a significant place in the history of our relationship with the bird. He suggests that, with the song's famous line, Maschwitz 'completed the process of nightingale mythification. At a stroke of his pen he removed the bird from nature and consigned it to an imaginary world as a magic creature existing on the same plane as angels in restaurants.'[38] While McCarthy acknowledges the romanticized nightingale already had a place in literary history, he argues that Maschwitz completed nightingale 'mythification', contributing to the 'living nightingale's eclipse', in conjunction with the disappearance of real birdsong from our lives.[39] Yet events such as Sam Lee's Extinction Rebellion finale show how cultural history can also return that which has been lost, a rewilding through song ultimately leading to the return of the living creature to our lives and green spaces. Prior to the arrival of the singing protestors, a nightingale had already landed in Berkeley Square in spring 2019 by way of a mural that formed part of the 'Lost Birds' project by street artist ATM, who uses his art to communicate the extinction crisis. The nightingale was painted on the tailplane of a Vickers Wellington bomber that had been brought to the square, in homage to the BBC nightingale broadcast of 1942. The mural was filmed as part of the documentary *Last Song of the Nightingale*, a crowdfunded project by Sunbittern Media, which brings attention to the plight of the bird in reference to its science, culture and ecology. Spring 2019 also marked the bicentenary of the composition of Keats's 'Ode to a Nightingale' – featured in the documentary – and saw nightingales make it to the top twenty singles chart by way of the RSPB's 'Let Nature Sing'.

Poetry and environment also intersect in the way poems make for important historical nightingale records, rendered elegiac in the present day as their settings fall silent. Coleridge's 'The Nightingale'

Nightingale from Will Rose's animation for the Sunbittern Media *Last Song of the Nightingale* Conservation Documentary, launched in 2020.

(1798) is the earliest record of the bird in Somerset and thus an important piece on avifauna. Right on the western fringe of the nightingale's range, Somerset has never been a nightingale strong-hold, and while nightingales may have been abundant on the Quantocks in the spring of 1798, you would be hard-pressed to hear one in the locale of Coleridge's poem in the present day, let alone the throng of 'so many nightingales' he describes in the nearby grove, 'stirring the air with . . . harmony'. Nightingales haven't been heard in Clare's Royce – latterly Rice – Wood since its oaks were felled in the 1960s. Richard Mabey writes movingly of the demise of Clare's blackthorn clumps and pulpit oaks, 'levelled and obliterated . . . in most of Clare's old spots there was not even the possibility of a nightingale'.[40] The nearest nightingale Mabey finds is 5 km (3 mi.) south of Helpston, 'at the very edge of Clare's . . . world'.[41] Keats's poem on a nightingale nesting in Hampstead, then a village outside the city, can be situated in the history of the bird's gradual retreat from central London. In his diary entry for 28 May 1667, Samuel Pepys recorded hearing the nightingale in Vauxhall Gardens, while in 1703, the site where Buckingham Palace is now located was described as 'a little wilderness of Blackbirds and Nightingales'.[42] In the eighteenth century, there are further records of nightingales being common in Fulham and singing regularly in the gardens of Marylebone.[43] By the late 1870s, the bird had ceased breeding in many central locations, yet it could still be heard occasionally in Regent's Park (there is no official record of the bird singing in Berkeley Square, but this data suggests it is possible, even likely).[44] The nightingale last nested on Hampstead Heath in 1899. While Keats's bird sings in ecstasy in his poem, by its end, the song has become a 'plaintive anthem', as the bird disappears into the next valley glade: 'Fled is that music'. The ode becomes an elegy: 'Adieu! adieu! thy plaintive anthem fades', as the bird's disappearance foreshadows its permanent retreat from Hampstead eight decades later, with London advancing outwards into surrounding villages and fields. Reading's nightingale poem fully articulates this elegiac suggestiveness.

Percy Bysshe Shelley's fragment 'The Woodman and the Nightingale' (composed *c.* 1820/21) might also respond to Keats. This poem is directly about the destruction of nightingale habitat, an environmental parable of sorts that recalls the felling of trees in Virgil's *Georgics*. In his anthology of nightingale poems from the period, Romantic poetry academic Duncan Wu writes that the poem is a Romantic 'acknowledgement of the relationship between mankind and the natural world, and its implied warning that we disregard that relationship at our peril'.[45] For me, this poem speaks to and interweaves the themes of love, loss, closeness and hope with which this chapter has been concerned. Shelley's natural world inspires love and joy, and the nightingale's song, happy again, becomes 'love / In every soul but one' – that of the titular woodman whose 'rough heart was out of tune'.[46] The wood-man is woefully disconnected from the natural world and its invocations of deep feeling, to the extent that he takes to axe and saw and 'kill[s] the tall treen' – man's depredations of nature.[47] The poem isn't a petition or a lament, and it is free from overt judgement. Shelley instead focuses on the felt power of the wild copse and the trees, the 'soul' embodied by wood-nymphs, who, 'where high branches kiss',

> Make a green space among the silent bowers
> Like the vast fane in a metropolis
> Surrounded by the columns and the towers
>
> All overwrought with branch-like traceries
> in which there is a religion . . .[48]

While the poem may be about one man's alienation from the natural world, and his sacrilegious act, it is, in a sense, overwritten by the deep feeling others – we, hearts attuned – experience within it. Perhaps that's what Romantic poetry, the apex of nightingale lore, rewritten as joy, does: it is able to transcend the cultural gulfs and violations that the nightingale elsewhere so often manifests.

John Clare wrote 'I Love to look on nature with a poetic feeling
. . . I love to see the nightingale in its hazel retreat,' and perhaps
it's in his writings that the nature–culture divide most readily
dissolves, male bird becoming female bird in the grammar of
poetic feeling.[49] In Shelley's poem, as in Clare's, it is poetry that
comes down on the side of joy and love, and which is able to write
our relationship with the natural world. Shelley's poetic lines,
nearly always enjambed, even suggest the formation of the kiss-
ing branches, the 'branch-like traceries / in which there is a
religion'. This poem is a green space rewilded with 'unkindled
melodies' – those of the poet, singing the nightingale back to it.
'The poet is a nightingale,' wrote Shelley. He also wrote that poets
are 'the unacknowledged legislators of the world'. Its tragic violations notwithstanding, 'The Woodman and the Nightingale' is
a powerful and hopeful poem, through which we might legislate
our future relationship with this bird, with 'love / In every soul'.

Timeline of the Nightingale

c. 115,000 – c. 11,700 YEARS AGO

Common and thrush nightingale become separate species

10,000 YEARS AGO

Fossils suggest common nightingale arrives in the UK

4TH CENTURY BC

Aristotle mistakenly notes that both the male and female bird sing, in *History of Animals*

1798

Samuel Taylor Coleridge's 'The Nightingale' is published in *Lyrical Ballads*

1808

Beethoven's 'Pastoral Symphony' is first performed

1819

John Keats composes 'Ode to a Nightingale' in a Hampstead garden

1924

First BBC live broadcast of Beatrice Harrison duetting with the nightingale; Max Ernst collage, *Two Children are Threatened by a Nightingale* is made

1940

'A Nightingale Sang in Berkeley Square', sung by Vera Lynn, is released on record

1960S

Records show the nightingale population beginning to decline rapidly in the UK

AD 8	AD 77–9	1597
Ovid's *Metamorphoses* formalizes the Philomela myth	Pliny the Elder's *Natural History* includes a celebrated description of the nightingale's song	William Shakespeare's plays *Romeo and Juliet* and *The Merchant of Venice* designate the nightingale as a bird that sings at night only

1833	1843	1888	1911
John Clare's 'The Nightingales Nest' is published	Hans Christian Andersen's 'The Nightingale' is published	Oscar Wilde's 'The Nightingale and the Rose' is published	First record of the thrush nightingale in the UK

2014	2019	
Plans to build on Lodge Hill, a hugely important site for nightingales, prompt a huge RSPB campaign	Two-hundredth anniversary of John Keats's 'Ode to a Nightingale'; Sunbittern Media documentary *Last Song of the Nightingale* is crowd-funded and filmed; Berkeley Square is 'rewilded' with nightingale song at an Extinction Rebellion event	

References

INTRODUCTION: 'NO BETTER DRESS THAN RUSSET BROWN'

1 John Clare, 'The Nightingales Nest', in *Major Works*,
   ed. Eric Robinson and David Powell (Oxford, 1984), pp. 213–14.
2 James Bolton, *Harmonia Ruralis; or, An Essay Towards a Natural
   History of British Song Birds*, 2 vols (Manchester, 1794), vol. II,
   p. 52.
3 P. B. Shelley, 'A Defence of Poetry', *Shelley's Poetry and Prose*,
   ed. S. Reiman and J. Powers (London, 1977), p. 486.
4 This has been pointed out by bird folklorists such as Edward
   A. Armstrong and Francesca Greenoak. Greenoak notes in her
   survey of British bird lore, *All the Birds of the Air* (London, 1979),
   p. 29, that the bird 'would hardly deserve mention here were it not
   for its eminence in literary traditions'.
5 Sappho, '67', in *Poems and Fragments*, trans. Stanley Lombardo
   (Indianapolis, IN, 2002), n.p.; Geoffrey Chaucer, 'The Parliament
   of Fowls', in *Dream Visions and Other Poems*, ed. Helen Philips and
   Nick Havely (Harlow, Essex, 1997), p. 253.
6 John Keats, 'Ode to a Nightingale', in *The Oxford Authors: John
   Keats*, ed. Elizabeth Cook (Oxford, 1990), p. 288.
7 Samuel Taylor Coleridge, 'The Nightingale; A Conversation Poem,
   Written in April, 1798', in *Lyrical Ballads*, ed. R. L Brett and
   A. R. Jones, 2nd edn (London, 1991), p. 41.
8 Rev. C. A. Johns, *British Birds in their Haunts* (London, 1885), p. 123.
9 Ibid.
10 D. H. Lawrence, 'The Nightingale', *Forum* (September 1927),
   pp. 384–5.

11 'Luscinia', in *Oxford Latin Dictionary*, ed. P.G.W. Glare, 2 vols (Oxford, 1982), vol. I, p. 1069.

12 Anonymous, '8', *The Exeter Book of Riddles*, trans. Kevin Crossley-Holland (Harmondsworth, 1970), p. 30.

13 William Shakespeare, *The Oxford Shakespeare: The Complete Works*, ed. John Jowlett, William Montgomery, Gary Taylor and Stanley Wells, 2nd edn (Oxford, 2005), p. 389.

14 Ibid., p. 477.

15 Izaak Walton, *The Compleat Angler* (New York, 1996), p. 13.

16 On 'Thin Places', see Eric Weiner, 'Where Heaven and Earth Come Closer', *New York Times*, 9 March 2012, www.nytimes.com.

17 Edward Armstrong, *The Folklore of Birds* (New York, 1970), p. 187.

18 Anonymous, 'The Anti-nightingale Song', trans. Fleur Adcock, *The Virgin and the Nightingale* (Newcastle upon Tyne, 1988), p. 31.

19 Ibid.

20 Sir Edward Grey, *The Charm of Birds* (London, 1921), p. 65.

21 Richard Mabey, *The Book of Nightingales* (London, 1997), pp. 18–19. The work was originally published as *Whistling in the Dark* in 1993.

22 Mark Cocker, *Birds and People* (London, 2013), p. 423.

23 Aldhelm, *Aldhelm: The Poetic Works*, trans. Michael Lapidge and James L. Rosier (Cambridge, 2009), p. 74.

24 Anonymous, *The Owl and the Nightingale: Text and Translation*, trans. Neil Cartlidge (Liverpool, 2003), p. 15.

25 Pliny the Elder, *Natural History*, trans. H. Rackham (Cambridge, MA, 2014), p. 345.

26 Anonymous, '8', *The Exeter Book Riddles*, p. 30.

27 Pliny the Elder, *Natural History*, p. 345.

28 Mabey, *The Book of Nightingales*, pp. 8–9.

29 Richard Mabey, 'Nature's Voyeurs', *The Guardian*, 15 March 2003, www.theguardian.co.uk.

30 Tony Pinkney, 'Romantic Ecology', in *A Companion to Romanticism*, ed. Duncan Wu (Malden, 2001), p. 414; Tim Dee, *Landfill* (London, 2018), p. 65. See Dee's discussion of naming,

distancing and nature-capture as love more widely in *Landfill*,
pp. 63–6, which has influenced my thinking.

31   Keats, 'Ode to a Nightingale', in *The Oxford Authors*, p. 289.

1 NATURAL HISTORY NIGHTINGALES: 'WHEN THE BUDS OF THE
LEAVES ARE SWELLING'

1   The main sources of ornithological information for this chapter
are Peter Clement, *Robins and Chats* (London, 2005); Stanley
Cramp, ed., *Handbook of the Birds of Europe, the Middle East and
North Africa*, vol. v: *The Birds of the Western Palearctic: Tyrant
Flycatchers to Thrushes* (Oxford, 1988); and Andy Brown and Phil
Grice, *Birds in England* (London, 2005).

2   BirdLife International, '*Luscinia megarhynchos* (Common
Nightingale) Supplementary Material', *European Red List of Birds*
(2015), http://datazone.birdlife.org.

3   Brown and Grice, *Birds in England*, p. 477.

4   Georges Louis Leclerc, Comte de Buffon, *Natural History of Birds,
Fish, Insects and Reptiles*, trans. William Smellie, 5 vols (London,
1793), vol. v, pp. 99–100.

5   Samuel Taylor Coleridge, *Lyrical Ballads*, ed. R. L Brett and A. R.
Jones, 2nd edn (London, 1991), p. 42; T. S. Eliot, 'The Waste Land',
The Complete Poems and Plays (London, 1969), p. 64.

6   Oliver Pike, *The Nightingale: Its Story and Song* (London, 1932),
p. 18.

7   Michael Weiss, Sarah Kiefer and Silke Kipper, 'Buzzwords in
Females' Ears? The Use of Buzz Songs in the Communication of
Nightingales (*Lusciinia megarhynchos*)', *PLOS ONE*, VII/9 (September
2012), no pagination.

8   David Rothenberg, *Nightingales in Berlin: Searching for the Perfect
Sound* (London and Chicago, IL, 2019), pp. 46–7.

9   Ibid., p. 46.

10   Ibid., pp. 6 and 48.

11   Pike, *The Nightingale*, pp. 23–4.

12   British Trust for Ornithology, 'Managing Scrub for Nightingales'
Leaflet (2015).

13 Ibid.
14 Clement, *Robins and Chats*, p. 262.
15 Ibid.
16 Paul Stancliffe, 'Tagged!', in *Birdwatching* (2011), available at
    www.bto.org, pp. 68–70.
17 Mike Dilger, *Nightingales in November* (London, 2016), p. 108.
18 Pliny the Elder, *Natural History*, trans. H. Rackham (Cambridge,
    MA, 2014), p. 345.
19 John Ray, *The Ornithology of Francis Willughby of Middleton in the
    County of Warwick, esq. . . .* (London, 1678), p. 220.
20 Buffon, *Natural History of Birds*, pp. 79–80.
21 Thomas Pennant, *British Zoology*, 4 vols (London, 1768), vol. II,
    pp. 255–6.
22 George Montagu, 'Nightingale', in *Ornithological Dictionary; or,
    Alphabetical Synopsis of British Birds*, 2 vols (London, 1802), vol. I.
23 John Gould, *The Birds of Europe* (London, 1837), vol. II, n. p.
24 Daines Barrington, 'XXXI. Experiments and Observations on the
    Singing of Birds', *Philosophical Transactions: Giving Some Account
    of the Present Undertakings, Studies, and Labours, of the Ingenious,
    in many Considerable Parts of the World* (London, 1773), vol. LXIII,
    part i, pp. 249 and 281.
25 Ibid., p. 284.
26 Ibid., p. 282.
27 Quoted in Ray, *The Ornithology of Francis Willughby*, p. 221.
28 Giovanni Pietro Olina, *Uccelliara*, trans. Kate Clayton as *Pasta
    for Nightingales: A 17th-century Handbook of Bird-care and Folklore*,
    ed. Sarah Kane (London, 2018), p. 75.
29 Ibid., p. 69.
30 The title is also given to a French film by Jean Fléchet, 1970 –
    an opera with themes of birdsong, sleep and dreaming.
31 T. R. Birkhead and I. Charmantierb, 'Nicolas Venette's *Traité du
    Rossignol* (1697) and the Discovery of Migratory Restlessness',
    Archives of Natural History, XL/1 (April 2013), p. 135.
32 Ray, *The Ornithology of Francis Willughby*, p. 222.
33 Charlotte Smith, *The Works of Charlotte Smith*, ed. Stuart Curran,
    14 vols (London, 2005–7), vol. XIII, p. 334.

34 Charlotte Smith, 'On the Departure of the Nightingale', in
    The Works of Charlotte Smith, vol. XIV, p. 21.
35 Johann Matthäus Bechstein, *The Natural History of Cage Birds: Their
    Management, Habits, Food, Diseases* . . . (London, 1835), p. 207.
36 Ibid.
37 *Gentleman's Magazine*, 22 (1752), p. 219.
38 William Yarrell, *A History of British Birds*, 3 vols, 2nd edn (London,
    1845), vol. I, p. 303.
39 John Burroughs, *Fresh Fields* (Edinburgh, 1893), p. 156.
40 Ibid., p. 157.
41 Smith, *Works*, vol. XIII, p. 334.

2 LITERARY NIGHTINGALES: 'OLD-WORLD PAIN'

 1 Matthew Arnold, *Poems by Matthew Arnold* (London, 1885),
    p. 46.
 2 Homer, *The Odyssey of Homer*, trans. Richmond Lattimore
    (New York, 1999), p. 295.
 3 Aristophanes, *The Birds and Other Plays*, trans. David Barrett and
    Alan H. Sommerstein (London, 2003), p. 177.
 4 Virgil, *Georgics*, trans. Peter Fallon (Oxford, 2006), p. 92.
 5 Ibid.
 6 Ovid, *Metamorphoses*, trans. A. D. Melville (Oxford, 1986), p. 142.
 7 Margaret Atwood, 'Nightingale', in *The Tent* (London, 2006),
    p. 138.
 8 Pausanias, *Pausanias's Description of Greece*, trans. J. G. Frazer,
    6 vols (London, 1898), vol. I, p. 63.
 9 Paulinus of Nola, untitled poem in 'Appendix II: Christian Latin
    Poems', in Jeni Williams, *Interpreting Nightingales: Gender, Class
    and Histories* (Sheffield, 1997), p. 241.
10 Anonymous, 'Love's Agent', trans. Fleur Adcock, *The Virgin and
    the Nightingale* (Newcastle upon Tyne, 1988), p. 29.
11 Ibid.
12 Bernart de Ventadorn, 'Can l'erba fresch e-lh folha par', in *Songs of
    Bernart de Ventadorn*, ed. Stephen G. Nichols Jr and John A. Galm
    (Chapel Hill, NC, 1962), p. 154.

13 Marie de France, *The Lais of Marie de France*, trans. Glyn S. Burgess and Keith Busby (London, 1986), p. 95.

14 Giovanni Boccaccio, *The Decameron*, trans. Guido Waldman (Oxford, 1993), p. 343.

15 Ibid.

16 Anonymous, *The Owl and the Nightingale: Text and Translation*, trans. Neil Cartlidge (Liverpool, 2003), pp. 14–15.

17 Ibid., p. 15.

18 Ibid., p. 5.

19 Confusingly, *bulbul* is also applied to members of the *Pycnonotidae* family, so some *bulbul* poems are about different species altogether.

20 Farid Ud-Din Attar, *The Conference of Birds*, trans. Afkham Darbandi and Dick Davis (London, 1984), p. 36.

21 Hafez, *The Nightingales Are Drunk*, trans. Dick Davis (London, 2015), p. 35.

22 Sir Philip Sidney, 'Certain Sonnets: 4 To the Same Tune', *The Major Works*, ed. Katherine Duncan-Jones (Oxford, 1989), pp. 15–16.

23 William Shakespeare, 'The Rape of Lucrece', in *The Oxford Shakespeare: The Complete Works*, ed. John Jowlett, William Montgomery, Gary Taylor and Stanley Wells, 2nd edn (Oxford, 2005), p. 249.

24 John Milton, *The Complete Poems*, ed. John Leonard (London, 1998), p. 171.

25 Ibid.

26 Joseph Warton, 'Ode IX. To the Nightingale', in *Odes on Various Subjects* (London, 1746), p. 34.

27 John Aikin, *An Essay on the Application of Natural History to Poetry* (London, 1777), p. 33.

28 Ibid.

29 James Thomson, 'Spring', *Poetical Works*, ed. J. Logie Robertson (London, 1971), p. 25.

30 Ibid.

31 Samuel Taylor Coleridge, *Lyrical Ballads*, ed. R. L Brett and A. R. Jones, 2nd edn (London, 1991), p. 41.

32 Ibid., p. 42.
33 John Keats, letter to George and Georgiana Keats, February–
May 1819, in *The Oxford Authors: John Keats*, ed. Elizabeth Cook
(Oxford, 1990), p. 468.
34 John Keats, 'Ode to a Nightingale', in *The Oxford Authors*, p. 285.
35 Ibid., p. 287.
36 Ibid.
37 Richard Mabey, *The Book of Nightingales* (London, 1997), p. 77.
38 Keats, 'Ode to a Nightingale', p. 288.
39 Tim Dee, *The Running Sky* (London, 2009), p. 218.
40 John Clare, *The Natural History Prose Writings of John Clare*,
ed. Margaret Grainger (Oxford, 1983), p. 42.
41 Ibid., p. 38.
42 John Clare, *Major Works*, ed. Eric Robinson and David Powell
(Oxford, 1984), pp. 213–14.
43 Ibid.
44 John Clare, *The Letters of John Clare*, ed. Mark Storey (Oxford,
1985), p. 519.
45 Clare, *Natural History Prose Writings*, p. 313.
46 Coleridge, quoted by Brett and Jones in *Lyrical Ballads*, p. 279.

3 LITERARY NIGHTINGALES: 'SELFSAME SONG'

1 Christina Rossetti, *The Complete Poems of Christina Rossetti*
(London, 1979–90), vol. I, p. 52.
2 Matthew Arnold, *Poems by Matthew Arnold* (London, 1885), p. 47.
3 Rossetti, *The Complete Poems*, vol. I, p. 52, and vol. III, p. 178.
4 Alfred Lord Tennyson, 'In Memoriam A. H. H.', in *Selected Poems*,
ed. Christopher Ricks (London, 2007), p. 159.
5 Alfred Lord Tennyson, Note to *The Princess: A Medley* (London,
1908), p. 258.
6 Elizabeth Barrett Browning, *The Poetical Works of Elizabeth Barrett
Browning* (London, 1897), p. 526.
7 Hans Christian Andersen, 'The Nightingale', in *Hans Andersen:
His Classic Fairy Tales*, trans. Erik Haugaard (London, 1976), p. 19.
8 Ibid., p. 21.

9 Oscar Wilde, 'The Nightingale and the Rose', *The Classic Fairy Tales*, ed. Maria Tartar, 2nd edn (London, 2017), p. 261.

10 Ibid., pp. 262–3.

11 Ibid., p. 263.

12 Ibid., p. 265.

13 T. S. Eliot, *The Complete Poems and Plays* (London, 1969), p. 64.

14 Ibid.

15 Eliot, 'Sweeny among the Nightingales', in *Complete Poems*, p. 57.

16 Mina Loy, *Lunar Baedeker and Times-tables* (Highlands, NC, 1958), p. 80.

17 Jorge Luis Borges, 'To the Nightingale', in *To a Nightingale: Sonnets and Poems from Sappho to Borges*, ed. Edward Hirsch (New York, 2007), p. 44.

18 Ted Hughes, 'Keats', *Collected Poems*, ed. Paul Keegan (London, 2005), p. 128. As Hughes's letter to Marina Warner continues, 'Once in S. Yorks. rumour went through the school that there was a nightingale in some woodland near Conisbrough. (Rather as you now hear the 'beast' has been sighted in some copse round here.) Groups of enthusiasts were going out there. Eventually, I sat in there for a couple [of] hours and finally heard 3 piercing notes – but I swear they were the squeals of dry brakes in the shunting yard down below the wood'; see Marina Warner, *Signs and Wonders: Essays on Letters and Culture* (London, 2003), p. 444. The '3 piercing notes' resonates with the first line of his poem 'Keats': 'Once I heard three notes of a nightingale in a dark wood' (Hughes, *Collected Poems*, p. 128).

19 Wallace Stevens, *The Collected Poems of Wallace Stevens* (New York, 1954), p. 160.

20 Paul Muldoon, 'Nightingales', in *Hay* (London, 1998), p. 11.

21 Deryn Rees-Jones, 'Nightingale' (2019), reproduced by *The Guardian*, 7 March 2020, www.theguardian.com. The poem was commissioned to mark the bicentenary of the composition of Keats's ode, and appears in the Keats-Shelley Memorial Association's anthology *Odes for John Keats*, as well in postcard form as part of a Literature and Science hub project at University of Liverpool: www.liverpool.ac.uk.

22 W. S. Merwin, 'Night Singing', in *To a Nightingale: Sonnets and Poems from Sappho to Borges*, p. 45.

23 R. F. Langley, 'To a Nightingale', in *Complete Poems*, ed. Jeremy Noel-Tod (Manchester, 2015), p. 153. Quoted by kind permission of Carcanet Press Ltd, Manchester.

24 Ibid., pp. 153–4.

25 Anne Finch, 'A Nocturnal Rêverie', in *Miscellany Poems On Several Occasions* (London, 1713), p. 291; Anne Finch, 'To the Nightingale', in *Miscellany Poems*, p. 200.

26 Anne Finch, 'To the Nightingale', in *Miscellany Poems*, p. 200.

27 Margaret Atwood, 'Nightingale', in *The Tent* (London, 2006), p. 137.

28 Ibid., p. 138.

29 Paisley Rekdal, *Nightingale* (Port Townsend, WA, 2019), p. 54.

4 MUSICAL NIGHTINGALES: 'ORGAN OF DELIGHT'

1 See David Rothenberg, *Why Birds Sing: A Journey into the Mystery of Bird Song* (New York, 2005); and Hollis Taylor, *Is Birdsong Music?: Outback Encounters with an Australian Songbird* (Bloomington, IN, 2017).

2 Olavi Sotavalta, *Analysis of the Song Patterns of Two Sprosser Nightingales, Luscinia luscinia* (Helsinki, 1956).

3 Quoted in George Grove, *Beethoven and His Nine Symphonies* (Cambridge, 2014), p. 191.

4 Quoted in Anthony Pople, *Messiaen: Quatuor pour la fin du Temps* (Cambridge, 1998), p. 94.

5 Quoted in Daniel Albright, *Stravinsky: The Music Box and the Nightingale* (New York, 1989), p. 22.

6 The contrast is overridden in Stravinsky's later work 'Le chant du rossignol' (The Song of the Nightingale), a symphonic poem first performed in 1919 and adapted from *Le rossignol*, in which the real and mechanical nightingale are represented by solo flute and oboe, respectively. A ballet version premiered in 1920, choreographed by Leonid Massine with design by Henri Matisse.

7 Albright, *Stravinsky*, p. 22.

8   John Clare, *The Natural History Prose Writings of John Clare*,
    ed. Margaret Grainger (Oxford, 1983), p. 42.

9   Both bird and human share the instrument of voice, of course,
    and both produce sounds in essentially the same way (the
    oscillations of the vocal cords in humans and the labia of the
    syrinx in birds), although the double-barrelled syrinx is greatly
    more complex than the larynx, of course, far exceeding human
    capability in its extraordinary range of high- and low-frequency
    notes. The name of the syrinx comes from the name of an ancient
    musical instrument also known as the panpipe, from which it's
    not too much of a step to other wind instruments that also work
    through vibration, able to direct human breath to higher pitches
    and nightingale-like passages and trills.

10 Michael Arlen, *These Charming People* (London, 1923), p. 15.

11 'A Nightingale Sang in Berkeley Square', words and music by
    Eric Maschwitz, Manning Sherwin © 1940. Reproduced with
    permission of Peter Maurice Music Co Ltd/EMI Music Publishing,
    London W1F 9LD.

12 'Visions of Johanna', written by Bob Dylan. Copyright © 1966 by
    Dwarf music; renewed 1994 by Dwarf Music. All rights reserved.
    International copyright secured. Reprinted by permission.
    'Jokerman', written by Bob Dylan. Copyright © 1983 by Special
    Rider Music. All rights reserved. International copyright secured.
    Reprinted by permission.

13 Beatrice Harrison, *The Cello and the Nightingales*, ed. Patricia
    Cleveland-Peck (London, 1985), p. 127.

14 Ibid., p. 133.

15 Sir John Reith, 'The Broadcasting of Silence', *Radio Times*, 6 June
    1924, p. 437.

16 According to this tale, the BBC had well-known bird impressionist
    Maude Gould – sometimes known as Madame Saberon – on
    standby in case the nightingale didn't show up. Jeremy Mynott
    put it to the test of two birding experts, who analysed the 1924
    nightingale recording in question: 'Both agreed it had curious
    structural and other features, but one of them concluded that it
    was probably a nightingale, and one that it probably wasn't'; see

Jeremy Mynott, *Birdscapes: Birds in Our Imagination and Experience* (Oxford, 2009), p. 317.

17 David Rothenberg, *Nightingales in Berlin: Searching for the Perfect Sound* (London and Chicago, IL, 2019), p. 10.

18 Ibid., p. 15.

19 Sam Lee, 'First Person: Sam Lee on Singing with Endangered Nightingales', 3 May 2019, https://theartsdesk.com.

20 Richard Mabey, *The Barley Bird: Notes on the Suffolk Nightingale* (Framlingham, Suffolk, 2010), p. 77.

21 David Hindley, 'The Music of Birdsong', *Wildlife Sound*, VI/4 (1990), p. 31.

22 Ibid.

5 'IMMORTAL BIRD'? NIGHTINGALES IN DECLINE

1 Aldous Huxley, *Literature and Science* (London, 1963), p. 94.

2 Ibid.

3 This is despite numbers increasing in some countries (Germany, Spain, Switzerland), and decreasing in others (Turkey, Belgium, Cyprus, Albania). BirdLife International 'European Red List of Birds' (Luxembourg, 2015), http://datazone.birdlife.org.

4 BirdLife International, 'Long-term Population Trend' leaflets 2013 and 2018, https://pecbms.info and www.ebcc.info. The latest report of the Pan-European Common Bird Monitoring Scheme (PECBMS) puts the long-time trend at a decrease of 67 per cent, belying a more alarming status than the 'moderate' category, and the ten-year trend at an increase of 3 per cent. The thrush nightingale is classed as being in long-term and short-term moderate decline, although figures between years are much more variable. The PECBMS figures for the thrush nightingale are a 33 per cent and 24 per cent decline respectively. PECBMS data from https://pecbms.info, accessed November 2020.

5 Isabella Tree, *Wilding* (London, 2018), p. 129.

6 Chas A. Holt, Chris M. Hewson and Robert J. Fuller, 'The Nightingale in Britain: Status, Ecology and Conservation Needs', *British Birds*, CV/4 (April 2012), pp. 172–87.

7 Tree, *Wilding*, p. 129.
8 A study of the effects of deer browsing on nightingale habitat was undertaken in Bradfield Woods in Suffolk, England, which has been under continuous traditional coppice management since 1252 and where, since the 1980s, a decrease in nightingale territories has coincided with a large increase in deer numbers. The study showed that nightingale densities were fifteen times higher in deer-fenced areas than grazed ones, and concluded that optimal habitat characteristics are likely to be affected by even moderate levels of deer browsing; see Chas A. Holt, Robert J. Fuller, Paul M. Dolman, 'Experimental Evidence that Deer Browsing Reduces Habitat Suitability for Breeding Common Nightingales *Luscinia megarhynchos*', *Ibis*, CLII/2 (April 2010), pp. 335–46.
9 Benedict Macdonald, *Rebirding: Rewilding Britain and its Birds* (Exeter, 2019), p. 101.
10 Ibid., p. 213.
11 Tree, *Wilding*, p. 190.
12 Justin Hoffman, *Irreplaceable* (London, 2019), p. 137.
13 Ibid., p. 14.
14 Quoted by Jim Pickard and George Parker, 'Cabinet Tensions Show on Growth', *Financial Times* (27 February 2013), p. 3.
15 A. M. Wilson, A.C.B. Henderson and R. J. Fuller, 'Status of the Nightingale *Luscinia megarhynchos* in Britain at the End of the 20th Century with Particular Reference to Climate Change', *Bird Study*, XLIX/3 (January 2002), pp. 193–204.
16 Ibid.
17 Carolina Remacha, César Rodríguez, Javier de la Puente and Javier Pérez-Tris, 'Climate Change and Maladaptive Wing Shortening in a Long-distance Migratory Bird', *The Auk*, CXXXVII/3 (1 July 2020), no pagination.
18 Holt et al., ''The Nightingale in Britain', p. 183.
19 Ibid.
20 Huxley, *Literature and Science*, pp. 94–5.
21 The crash in numbers of cuckoos in areas of England has been shown to be closely linked to declines in tiger moth caterpillars on which they feed, for example.

22 Mark Cocker, *Our Place: Can We Save Britain's Wildlife before It Is Too Late?* (London, 2018), p. 300; Robert Macfarlane, 'Generation Anthropocene: How Humans Have Altered the Planet for Ever', *The Guardian*, 1 April 2016, www.theguardian.com.

23 Peter Reading, untitled poem, in *Collected Poems 3: Poems, 1997–2003* (Tarset, Northumberland, 2003), p. 305.

24 Rachel Carson, *Silent Spring*, Fortieth Anniversary Edition (Boston, MA, 2002), p. 103.

25 Patrick Barkham, 'The Housing Development that Could Silence Our Nightingales', *The Guardian*, 6 June 2016, www.theguardian.com.

26 Ibid.

27 Helen Macdonald, 'Our Springs Grow Emptier as the Birdsong Falls Silent', *New Statesman*, 2 April 2015, www.newstatesman.com.

28 Ted Hughes, 'Tereus', *Tales from Ovid* (London, 1997), p. 245.

29 Virgil, *Georgics*, trans. Peter Fallon (Oxford, 2006), p. 34.

30 Despite the protection of law, nightingales are among the victims of the hundreds of species caught by nets on migration routes for the ancient 'delicacy' of *beccafico* (more traditionally, these are species of the Old World warbler family).

31 Oliver Pike, *The Nightingale: Its Story and Song* (London, 1932), p. 20.

32 Quoted in John Lewis-Stempel, *Where Poppies Blow: The British Soldier, Nature, the Great War* (London, 2016), p. 44.

33 Quoted ibid., p. 42.

34 James Thomson, *Poetical Works*, ed. J. Logie Robertson (London, 1971), pp. 29–30.

35 Ibid., p. 30.

36 Ibid.

37 Richard Jefferies, *Landscape with Figures: Selected Prose Writings*, ed. Richard Mabey (London, 2013), p. 99.

38 Michael McCarthy, *Say Goodbye to the Cuckoo* (London, 2009), p. 50

39 Ibid.

40 Mabey, *The Book of Nightingales*, p. 103.

41 Ibid.

42 Quoted by Andrew Self, *The Birds of London* (London, 2014),
   p. 343.
43 Ibid.
44 Ibid., p. 344.
45 Duncan Wu, 'Introduction', in *Immortal Bird: The Nightingale
   in Romantic Poetry*, ed. Duncan Wu (Rome, 2011), p. xiii.
46 Percy Bysshe Shelley, 'The Woodman and the Nightingale',
   in *Immortal Bird: The Nightingale in Romantic Poetry*,
   ed. Duncan Wu, pp. 35 and 33.
47 Ibid.
48 Ibid., p. 36.
49 John Clare, *The Natural History Prose Writings of John Clare*,
   ed. Margaret Grainger (Oxford, 1983), p. 38.

Select Bibliography

Armstrong, Edward, *The Folklore of Birds* (New York, 1970)

Brown, Andy, and Phil Grice, *Birds in England* (London, 2005)

Clarke, Hockley, *A Garland of Nightingales* (London, 1979)

Clement, Peter, *Robins and Chats* (London, 2005)

Cocker, Mark, *Birds and People* (London, 2013)

—, and Richard Mabey, *Birds Britannica* (London, 2005)

Cramp, Stanley, ed., *Handbook of the Birds of Europe, the Middle East and North Africa*, vol. V: *The Birds of the Western Palearctic: Tyrant Flycatchers to Thrushes* (Oxford, 1988)

Dee, Tim, *Running Sky* (London, 2009)

Dilger, Mike, *Nightingales in November* (London, 2016)

Fisher, James, *The Shell Bird Book* (London, 1966)

Greenoak, Francesca, *All the Birds of the Air: The Names, Lore, and Literature of British Birds* (London, 1979)

Groom, Nick, 'John Clare at Christmas: The Seasons and the English Calendar' [unpublished essay available in the form of a recorded lecture], 12 December 2014, https://researchsupporthub. northampton.ac.uk

Hartshorne, Charles, *Born to Sing: Interpretation and World Survey of Bird Song* (Bloomington, IN, 1973)

Haughton, Hugh, 'Progress and Rhyme: 'The Nightingale's Nest' and Romantic Poetry', in *John Clare in Context*, ed. Hugh Haughton, Adam Phillips and Geoffrey Summerfield (Cambridge, 1994), pp. 51–86

Hirsch, Edward, ed., *To a Nightingale: Sonnets and Poems from Sappho to Borges* (New York, 2007)

Keynes, Geoffrey, and Peter Davidson, eds, *A Watch of Nightingales*
 (London, 1981)
Mabey, Richard, *The Barley Bird: Notes on the Suffolk Nightingale*
 (Framlingham, Suffolk, 2010)
—, *The Book of Nightingales* (London, 1997)
Macdonald, Benedict, *Rebirding: Rewilding Britain and Its Birds*
 (Exeter, 2019)
Pfeffer, Wendy, *The Change of Philomel: The Nightingale in Medieval
 Literature* (New York, 1985)
Pike, Oliver, *The Nightingale: Its Story and Song* (London, 1932)
Rothenberg, David, *Nightingales in Berlin: Searching for the Perfect
 Sound* (London and Chicago, IL, 2019)
—, *Why Birds Sing: A Journey into the Mystery of Bird Song*
 (New York, 2005)
Tree, Isabella, *Wilding* (London, 2018)
Williams, Jeni, *Interpreting Nightingales: Gender, Class and Histories*
 (Sheffield, 1997)

Associations and Websites

BRITISH TRUST FOR ORNITHOLOGY
www.bto.org
'Species focus' page on the nightingale and information about the
BTO's important work on the bird.

FORSCHUNGSFALL NACHTIGALL
https://forschungsfallnachtigall.de
German website about the nightingale citizen science project in Berlin.

NIGHTINGALE NIGHTS
http://nightingalenights.org.uk
An excellent resource 'celebrating the magical songster', with a range
of nightingale information, poems and music.

NIGHTINGALES IN BERLIN
www.nightingalesinberlin.com
David Rothenberg's site detailing his extensive work with nightingales
in Berlin.

RSPB
www.rspb.org.uk
Information on the common nightingale, with video and audio. Also
includes history of the threat to and campaign to save Lodge Hill.

SINGING WITH NIGHTINGALES
https://thenestcollective.co.uk
The website for Sam Lee's Singing with Nightingales concerts.

Acknowledgements

I have amassed a huge debt of thanks in the making of such a small book, and am very grateful to many people for their kindness and generosity. As ever, my deepest thanks go to Paul Baines for his unceasing support and inspiration: as with all my work, this book wouldn't exist without him, and he has been a generous reader of drafts as well as a dearly appreciated mentor, colleague and – I hope he doesn't mind – friend. Special thanks also go to Tim Dee and David Rothenberg for their kindness and generosity, for tip-offs, for reading material and for inspiring and teaching me through their own work. A big thank you also to Isabella Tree for reading and advising on material in the final chapter. I am hugely grateful for the various support and advice of other colleagues in the Department of English, University of Liverpool, who include Matthew Bradley, Alex Broadhead, Danny O'Connor, Michael Davies, Natalie Hanna, David Hering, Greg Lynall, Sandeep Parmar, Deryn Rees-Jones, Jill Rudd and Sam Solnick, to name those whom I bothered most. I'm grateful also to the School of the Arts, and to the professional services staff there, for financial and administrative support. Dear thanks to the following assorted nightingale experts and enthusiasts, acquaintances, colleagues of sorts and friends: Anna Allum, Amy-Jane Beer, Tom Bonnett, Anna Burton, Mark Cocker, Bethan Collins, Mary Colwell, Sarah Darwin, Hunter Dukes, Peter Espé and Buzz, Alexandra Harris, Emma Hayward, Katy Hooper, Neal Johnson, Sallie Lambert (I can't thank her enough for all she's done for me), Dominic Lewington (for incomparable musical knowledge, as well as much-cherished support and belief), Bernadette McBride, Luke Massey, Richard Mabey (not only for an email exchange, but for how his book, *Whistling in the*

Dark, led the way), Anna Mercer, Stephen Moss, Robyn Orr, Richard Smyth, Katie Stacey, Kelly Sultzbach, Michael Warren, Sarah Westcott, Nick Wrigley (who helped enormously with the images) and John Wright. I am very grateful to Michael Leaman and Jonathan Burt at Reaktion Books for their patience and whose feedback and expertise has been invaluable. Thank you also to Alex Ciobanu, Amy Salter and Susannah Jayes at Reaktion, as well as to the copy-editor, proofreader and designer of this work. Thank you to the kind support of my local Liverpool RSPB group, the members of which have taught me much; special thanks to Chris Wall. Thank you to my dear parents Jill and Lloyd for their love and support; my brother Huw Roberts; Uncle Ian Condliffe; friends Anna Adams, Katy Taylor, Natalie Jones and Kathleen Fitzpatrick; as well as the Wrexham 'Tribe'. Last, but by no means least, thank you to Tom Rawlinson, Scotch Nightingale, for his support, for the happy delay to this book's completion, for giving it flight and for inspiring me anew.

PERMISSIONS

R. F. Langley, 'To a Nightingale', in *Complete Poems*, ed. Jeremy Noel-Tod (Manchester, 2015), p. 153, quoted by kind permission of Carcanet Press Ltd, Manchester. 'A Nightingale Sang in Berkeley Square', words and music by Eric Maschwitz, Manning Sherwin © 1940. Reproduced with the permission of Peter Maurice Music Co Ltd/EMI Music Publishing, London W1F 9LD. 'Visions of Johanna', written by Bob Dylan. Copyright © 1966 by Dwarf music; renewed 1994 by Dwarf Music. All rights reserved. International copyright secured. Reprinted by permission. 'Jokerman', written by Bob Dylan. Copyright © 1983 by Special Rider Music. All rights reserved. International copyright secured. Reprinted by permission.

Photo Acknowledgements

The author and publishers wish to express their thanks to the following sources of illustrative material and/or permission to reproduce it. Some locations are also supplied here for reasons of brevity.

Acme Whistles: p. 129; Alamy: pp. 46 (blickwinkel), 48 (WildPictures), 89 (Buiten-Beeld); photos courtesy of Anna Allum: pp. 148, 152; David Andrews, via Anna Allum: p. 103; Mike Beck, 2014, via Anna Allum: p. 62; Biodiversity Heritage Library: pp. 28, 30, 32, 39, 51, 54 left and right, 56, 97, 116, 139, 146; Bridgeman Images: pp. 12 (Accademia Italiana, London), 100 (© Look and Learn); British Trust for Ornithology: p. 44; Cleveland Museum of Art: p. 163; image courtesy of Patricia Cleveland-Peck: p. 141; www.comptoir-des-monnaies.com: p. 161; Stephen Daglish: p. 109; The Database of Mid-Victorian Illustrations (DMVI), Cardiff University: pp. 94, 112; Richard Edwards (www.edwardschina.co.uk): p. 107; photo courtesy of Madeleine Floyd: p. 159; The J. Paul Getty Museum: pp. 73, 114 (Digital images courtesy of the Getty's Open Content Program); by permission of University of Glasgow Library, Archives & Special Collections: p. 120; photo courtesy of Julian Hoffman: p. 155; Gareth Hughes, via Anna Allum with permission: p. 6; Gareth Hughes, 2014 via Anna Allum: p. 81; image courtesy of Keats House, City of London: p. 87; Cédric Le Borgne, with permission: p. 134; Library of Congress, Washington, DC: p. 98; by courtesy of The University of Liverpool Library (Special Collections and Archives): pp. 29 (SPEC Ryl P3 13), 37, 45, 60 (SPEC J24.59), 67 (OLDHAM 806), 83 (SPEC L45.19), 168 (SPECJ24.59); The Metropolitan Museum of Art, New York: pp. 11 (H. O. Havemeyer Collection, Bequest of Mrs. H. O. Havemeyer, 1929), 64–5,

Index

Page numbers in *italics* indicate illustrations